Our words are a powerful weapon—for good or for evil. To wield our weapons properly, we need to allow God to steer our speech, aligning our words with his will. Karen Ehman has given us an important tool in this quest. *Zip It* takes us on a 40-day devotional journey through the Bible, giving us biblical direction, questions for reflection, and a daily challenge to ponder as we discover what to say, God's way of saying it, and when we'd better just shut our mouths.

> DR. TONY EVANS, senior pastor, Oak Cliff Bible Fellowship, Dallas; founder, The Urban Alternative; former chaplain, Dallas Cowboys; chaplain, Dallas Mavericks; author, *Watch Your Mouth: Understanding the Power of the Tongue*

This 40-day challenge is just what I need to help me refocus and think through the words I say daily. Karen Ehman's biblical wisdom, mixed with practical insight and everyday applications, helps me see that I can do better. If I follow God's Word and think before I speak, I can learn to zip it and so can you! This is a must-read for all of us.

> COURTNEY JOSEPH, author and blogger, WomenLivingWell.org and GoodMorningGirls.org

Karen Ehman combines biblical depth and relational breadth, then wraps it all in practical application, making *Zip It* the complete package! In it, Karen has identified all the nuances of our speech, especially those with potential to harm, calling us out in the very kindest way, and offering hope for our wayward tongues. The right word in the right manner at the right moment has the power to transform lives. I'm so grateful to Karen for inviting us to a place of loveliness and grace with our words in a world that so desperately needs both.

> GLYNNIS WHITWER, Executive Director of Communications, Proverbs 31 Ministries; Senior Editor, *Encouragement for Today* online devotions; editor, *The NIV Real-Life Devotional Bible for Women*

A great follow-up to her book *Keep It Shut*, this practical and engaging devotional will convict and encourage you! We all need to tame the tongue, don't we? This practical help is exactly what we need to get us there!

SHAUNTI FELDHAHN, social researcher and
bestselling author, *For Women Only*

Karen has done it again! In her coffee-shop-chat style, Karen's latest devotional encourages us to use our words wisely. With her perfect blend of teaching and transparency, Karen leads with wisdom and wit. I felt convicted but hopeful that this is a change that is biblical *and* possible!

WHITNEY CAPPS, national speaker for Proverbs
31 Ministries and writer for their First 5 app

Few people use words wisely. Those who do are like a "rare jewel," as the Scriptures say (Proverbs 20:15). Short, insightful, and aimed at the heart, Karen Ehman's brand new devotional, *Zip It*, offers hope to those of us who want to be that "rare jewel." Powerful!

PATRICK AND RUTH SCHWENK, founders of
TheBetterMom.com and ForTheFamily.
org; coauthors, *For Better or For Kids*

In *Zip It*, Karen Ehman gives us a hard but needed 40-day challenge to practice using our tongue to heal and give life instead of as a weapon that hurts and kills. Her use of Scripture coupled with personal examples help us learn to use our words for the honor of God and the good of our neighbor. This is a much-needed challenge!

JENNIFER THORN, pastor's wife and blogger, jenthorn.com

I love *Zip It* because it provides practical and creative tools to help us weigh our words and align them with God's truth. Each day

Karen equips us with takeaways, lessons, and prayers to ensure the words we speak not only please the Lord but also bless and encourage others. I especially love her challenge to create a "word-robe" (a word wardrobe) within our hearts and fill it with biblical truths and promises tailored to meet our needs and circumstances.

WENDY BLIGHT, Proverbs 31 Ministries First
5 Writing Team; author, *I Know His Name:
Discovering Power in the Name of God*

With great application, personal insight, and humor, Karen Ehman dives into an area each one of us struggles with—our words! She has a way of taking touchy subjects, giving them a fresh perspective, and pointing us to grace-covered truth. What a perfect book at any age and stage of life!

CLARE SMITH, blogger, speaker, personal
coach, and trainer, ClareSmith.me

Our words are directly tied to the condition of our relationship with Jesus. The 40-challenge of *Zip It* arrives at a great time in the history of the world. Social media, circles of friendships, and family relationships are built and destroyed with the power of our words. *Zip It* is a great book that will help you have victory of your mouth! Take the challenge!

CHRISSIE DUNHAM, Global Director of Women's
Ministry, Prestonwood Baptist Church

Our words hold the power to make someone feel like a king or a pauper. This book will help you with "mouth management" so the ones closest to you will feel like royalty. Karen Ehman is a trusted guide who will teach you when to zip it and when to speak up.

ARLENE PELLICANE, Proverbs 31 Ministries writer and
speaker; author, *31 Days to Becoming a Happy Mom*

Our words just may be the single most important key to successful relationships. This book is a gem and it reminds us of that. It's practical, easy-to-read, and just what is needed to enable us to use our words in a way that brings life to those around us. Thank you, Karen, for such a powerful book wives and husbands both can use!

> JILL SAVAGE, founder, Hearts at Home; coauthor with
> husband Mark Savage, *No More Perfect Marriages*

Karen Ehman teaches God's truth in an authentic, practical, humorous, yet very relational way. In her new book, *Zip It*, Karen guides us through Scriptures concerning the tongue, while also providing application-oriented takeaways and helpful lessons for our lips. Not only did *Zip It* inspire me to choose my words more carefully and prayerfully—especially when Facebook makes me feisty—but I also can't wait to read it with my two tween daughters. This devotion will be a "go-to" for many years to come. Highly recommend!

> CINDY BULTEMA, Bible teacher, speaker; and
> author, *Red Hot Faith* and *Live Full, Walk*
> *Free: Set Apart in a Sin-Soaked World*

Keeping my mouth shut is a daily struggle—whether it's talking too much when I need to listen, partaking in the watercooler gossip when I should walk away, writing my opinion on social media when it's not needed, or the hundreds of other reasons. While doing the *Keep It Shut* study I became more aware of my mouth and its actions. I am so excited for this devotional and the daily reminders of how to keep it shut! I have a feeling I will start it over every 40 days!

> MANDY YOUNG, speaker and blogger at MandyYoung.com

Thank you, Karen Ehman, for writing this book! *Zip It* landed in my lap when I absolutely needed to read it. Let me confess, as a woman who speaks far faster than she thinks; this 40-day challenge was a Godsend! With all the different relationships I juggle, I've witnessed far too many times how my words speak life or death. I'm so grateful for the truth and transformation found in these pages . . . and so are those closest to me!

MARIAN JORDAN ELLIS, author and
founder, Redeemed Girl Ministries

Imagine what the world would look like if we only used words to build, bless, encourage, and praise? That is the world Karen offers us through her compelling and life-giving challenge to zip it. This book is a much-needed 40-day diet for the soul—leaving you with new and life changing habits on how to use your words!

TRACY WILDE, speaker and author,
Finding the Lost Art of Empathy

Also by Karen Ehman

Keep It Shut: What to Say, How to Say It, and When to Say Nothing at All

Hoodwinked: Ten Myths Moms Believe & and Why We All Need to Knock It Off

Pressing Pause: 100 Quiet Moments for Moms to Meet with Jesus

Let. It. Go.: How to Stop Running the Show and Start Walking in Faith

Listen, Love, Repeat: Other-Centered Living in a Self-Centered World

ZIP IT

THE **KEEP IT SHUT**
40-DAY CHALLENGE

KAREN EHMAN

ZONDERVAN

Zip It
Copyright © 2017 by Karen Ehman

Requests for information should be addressed to:
Zondervan, *3900 Sparks Dr. SE, Grand Rapids, Michigan 49546*

ISBN 978-0-310-34587-9 (softcover)

ISBN 978-0-310-34504-8 (ebook)

Published in association with The Fedd Agency, P.O. Box 341973, Austin, TX 78734.

Art direction: Curt Diepenhorst
Interior design: Denise Froehlich

First printing December 2016/Printed in the United States of America

21 LSCH 10 9 8 7 6

To my father
Howltan Wayne "Pat" Patterson
You passed on to me your gift of gab but
also your habit of daily reading God's Word.
My love for you is beyond measure.

CONTENTS

Week Four: Taming Our Tempers

Week Five: Bad Speech/Good Speech

Week Six: When to Be Silent and When to Speak Up

Week Seven: Making Our Words Both Sweet and Salty

Week Eight: How God's Words Affect Our Words

INTRODUCTION

Words. Each day we use thousands of them in dozens of places. We utter them to our family members. We speak them at work. We strike up a conversation with a complete stranger or reply to our nosy neighbor. We ask a question of our child's teacher or patiently answer a toddler's question for the fifth time. And in addition to the words that roll off our lips, we have the ones we type with our fingertips—in the text, blog comment, or social media reply.

One thing is certain when it comes to our words: they are powerful and they have consequences. They can encourage or embitter, bless or badger, build up or break down. The tongue has the power of life and death (Prov. 18:21). Many times my words have been less than lovely, bringing about guilt and causing regret or even ushering in the death of a relationship. In fact, as I surveyed my life a few years ago, I observed that I could tether almost every tense or fractured relationship I'd had back to something I'd said. As God began to deal with me about the way I used my words, I learned to apply the vast advice the Bible has for us about how we should—and should not—speak. This led to my writing the book *Keep It Shut: What to Say, How to Say It, and When to Say Nothing at All*.

Since writing *Keep It Shut*, I have heard from countless

people about their own struggles with their words. Rarely a week goes by that I don't get an email or comment on social media from someone who has read the book and is trying to go down a new path, using their words for good and for God. But I am also often asked if I would consider writing more on the subject, providing some practical ways to implement the Bible's advice when it comes to how we speak to those in our lives.

The result of these requests is the book you now hold in your hands. It is my prayer that you will use it as a tool to dive deep into Scripture, discovering its relevant advice that can enable your interactions with others and your relationships to be at their very best.

The book is arranged in eight chapters on various themes that relate to our words, such as anger, when to be silent, when to speak up, and how to make our words both salty and sweet. The five entries within each chapter are designed for you to use Monday through Friday over an eight-week period.

The forty short entries each provide a challenge Scripture for the day and a story or example that helps to punctuate its theme. The "Today's Takeaways" section presents one or more bullet point nuggets to ponder for the day. The "Lesson for the Lips" feature gives practical challenges and doable activities to empower you to effectively live out the truths of Scripture. Each entry also concludes with a focused prayer.

Please know I will be continuing alongside you in this lifelong quest to temper our tongues, cheering you on all along the way. My prayer is that both of us will purpose to make our thoughts align with Scripture so when they turn into words they are pleasing to God and a gift to those who are listening.

Are you ready? Then turn to Day 1 as together we discover what we should say, how best to say it, and when we might better just zip it!

In Christ,

Karen

The Power of Our Words

1

A MATTER OF LIFE
AND DEATH

Death and life are in the power of the tongue, and those
who love it will eat its fruits. (Prov. 18:21 ESV)

I have learned something in my decades of relationships on
this earth: words are powerful, and they have consequences.

Words have always set events into motion. Often what
we have read about in our history books or experienced in
our own lives came about because of someone's speech.
Combative words have sparked wars, bringing about death
and destruction. Soothing words have calmed souls, quieted
hearts, and prevented potentially volatile situations from
escalating and producing dire consequences. Encouraging
words have imparted bravery and empowered doubting souls
to accomplish what they never dreamed they could. Loving
words have birthed relationships and bonded soul mates.

Can you think back on your own life and find evidence

of the power and lasting impact of words someone said either to or about you? I know I can. These phrases echo in the chambers of my mind and recall for me either pain and sorrow or love and inspiration.

When a neighborhood mom told my mother I was a "bossy child" who "acts like the mother hen of the subdivision," it hurt my heart. It made me think from an early age that my large-and-in-charge personality was a detriment and that no one really liked me; they were just tolerating me. So I longed instead to be a quiet-as-a-mouse little girl like Patti, a girl who lived behind me. But try as I might, I couldn't be meek and mild, let alone quiet.

When I was in college, a campus instructor made a comment to my face about my weight. (At that time I was about ten pounds over my doctor's recommended weight for my height and age.) I allowed her words to cling to my consciousness. And I wrongly surmised that any rejection I ever felt was because of my weight. If a guy dumped me, it was because I was fat. If I didn't get invited to an afternoon of shopping at the mall with girls in my dorm, it was because they didn't want to be seen with a heavy girl. Sometimes I even combined both of the hurtful phrases from my past, attributing rejection to the notion that I must be one bossy, obese gal!

But thankfully—although a little less often—words have been spoken to or about me that have lifted my spirits and from which I could draw strength, sometimes even decades later!

My seventh-grade English teacher wrote on one of my progress reports, "Karen is an excellent writer—especially with poetry." Later one of my college professors told a colleague how much I would be missed when I graduated because I took my jobs as a resident assistant, sports editor of the school paper, and director of the campus's social life activities very seriously. Yet another voice from my past echoes still to this day. As I discussed my uncertain future with a church staff member I knew in high school one day, she told me, "You will go far. I believe in you."

Yes, words are powerful and they have consequences. The consequences may be stellar—or sorrowful. They may be amazing—or awful. They may make an impact on lives for the better—or affect souls for the worse. Proverbs goes so far as to assert that "Death and life are in the power of the tongue" (18:21 ESV).

As we begin this 40-day journey together, we have a choice. We can use our speech—both spoken and written—for good or for evil. Our words can bring life-giving refreshment or deal a deathblow. Words can be warmth or a weapon. How we wield them will affect not only our relationships with others but our relationship with God.

Let's vow to learn all we can in these forty days to align our words with God's holy Word. Are you ready to begin? Your speech can help to change someone's world for the better, writing a story of love and peace.

Today's Takeaways

- *Words are like superglue.* Remember the old childhood chorus "Sticks and stones may break my bones, but words can never hurt me"? What a lie! We may have felt a tad better responding to our playground enemies with this chant, but we knew better. The truth is that bruises fade and bones eventually heal, but a scorched heart may take years to heal. Words stick. And not just sorta stick, like the creamy white school glue we used in third grade. They are more like superglue, nearly permanent and painful to peel off. This week, think about the truth that words stick. Before you lash out at someone in anger or leak a little sarcasm from your lips, remind yourself that your words have not only power for good or evil, they also have staying power.

- *We have a choice. Choose wisely.* Be choosey. Don't let words tumble off your tongue haphazardly or flippantly. Select your speech shrewdly. Craft your emails, texts, and social media posts and comments with care. A moment of cautious thought now can save boatloads of misunderstanding and pain later. Be conscientious, not careless. Impart life; don't dole out death.

Lesson for the Lips

Think back over your life. Does a phrase either spoken directly to you or said about you still echo in your mind today? Perhaps it was encouraging and brought life. Or maybe it was critical, caustic, or cutting and has stuck with you over the years, leaving an ache in your heart or pain in your soul. What words have stuck with you over the years? How does thinking about their lasting impact shape your perspective on how you use your own words with others today?

Prayer

Father, your Word tells us words are powerful and they have consequences. Make this truth stay close to me this week as I use my words to interact with others. I want to speak life into my relationships and not utter words that bring about death. May my speech glorify you today. In Jesus's name, amen.

2

THE GREAT KNOW-IT-ALL

Before a word is on my tongue you, Lord,
know it completely. (Ps. 139:4)

For the first decade of my marriage, I was involved in working with teenagers. My husband was a youth pastor and I was a volunteer in the junior and senior high youth program at church. This work included lots of Bible teaching and teen counseling but also the weekly duties of snack making and game organizing. One of the kids' favorite games was a little show my husband and I put on. I refer to it as "The Great Know-It-All."

In this little amusement, my husband would leave the room for a few minutes while I chose one of the teens to play the game. That teenager would select an object in the room to be "it." It might be the clock on the wall, a book on the shelf, one of the girls' purses, or a can of soda pop on the snack table. Then my husband would rejoin us. I would go around the room pointing at various objects, asking him, "Is this it? How about this? Is this it?" Every time, without fail, my husband was able to correctly guess which item the teenager had chosen.

This little shenanigan completely dumbfounded the kids. No matter how many times we did it, they never could figure out how my husband knew which item had been selected. (Hint: It had to do with what item I pointed to *before* pointing to the one selected and not at all with the one they'd chosen. And no, I will not divulge the secret of "The Great Know-It-All!")

Psalm 139 paints a breathtaking portrait of how intimately God knows us. Long ago he saw us as we were being formed in our mothers' wombs (vv. 13–16). And today he is acquainted with our daily activities, knowing when we sit down or stand up (v. 2). Why, God knows what we're going to say long before we even say it! Verse 4 boldly states, "Before a word is on my tongue you, LORD, know it completely." I observe two astonishing things tucked inside this verse.

First, God knows our words long before they ever leave our lips, before they are even on our tongues. This means he also knows the thoughts we are mulling in our minds. In fact, in Psalm 139:2, we are told God understands our thoughts even from far away. Before words are uttered audibly, they first originate in our minds. Thoughts turn into words.

Second, this verse shows us God not only knows the words we are about to speak, but that he knows them *completely*. He doesn't merely have an inkling of what we might say, but rather he thoroughly and completely knows what words have formed in our minds and are about to leak out of our mouths.

What a sobering verse to ponder! God really is the Great Know-It-All. He knows what we are thinking. He knows what we are about to say. He understands and ascertains us completely. No one is more intimately acquainted with our communications.

Today's Takeaways

- *Know your nakedness.* The truth of Psalm 139:4 should startle us a bit. Often—before our thoughts have formed into words and actually proceeded from our mouths—we think we can hide what we've been thinking. All the times I thought something unkind and longed to say it, but held back, I thought I had scored a major victory. But guess what! God still knows those thoughts. All our ways are laid bare before him. We can't hide. Our minds are naked before him. This should cause us to try to rein in our thoughts and keep them in line with God's Word. We may be able to hide from others, but we cannot hide from God.

- *Ponder what is pure.* Philippians 4:8 reads, "Brothers and sisters, whatever is true, whatever is noble, whatever is right, whatever is pure, whatever is lovely, whatever is admirable—if anything is excellent or praiseworthy—think about such things." God sure stresses the importance of our thought life. We are to ponder what is pure rather than let our thoughts paddle around in pollution. The best way to think of what is right, pure, lovely, and admirable is to meditate on Scripture. When our thoughts are in alignment with God's Word, our speech has a better chance at being uplifting, wholesome, and godly.

Lesson for the Lips

Today, let's not focus on our words so much but rather on our thought life. How would you rate your thinking on the following scale?

1—I often have less-than-lovely thoughts about others and even plot to do evil.

2—I occasionally have less-than-lovely thoughts about others and only sometimes plan to do wrong.

3—My thought life is a pretty even mix of good and evil.

4—Most of the time my thoughts are uplifting and godly and only occasionally do I struggle with keeping them in line.

5—I really don't have trouble keeping my thoughts in alignment with Scripture.

Now, to help keep your thought life in order, choose one of the verses mentioned here and try to memorize it this week. Write it on a sticky note and post it in a prominent place where you will see it often. Or type it out on your cell phone and make it your lock screen. Continue mentally rehearsing it, and even saying it out loud, until you memorize it. Then, in the future, when your thoughts want to migrate to a place where they will not be pleasing to God, quote the verse out loud.

- Psalm 139:4: "Before a word is on my tongue you, LORD, know it completely."

- Philippians 4:8: "Brothers and sisters, whatever is true, whatever is noble, whatever is right, whatever is pure, whatever is lovely, whatever is admirable—if anything is excellent or praiseworthy—think about such things."

Prayer

Heavenly Father, I know I cannot hide from you. I cannot hide my words nor even my thoughts. May I be mindful today to bring both my words and my thoughts into line with your Word so they will be pleasing in your sight. In Jesus's name, amen.

3

SHUTTING DOWN THE MOTORMOUTH

When there are many words, transgression and offense
are unavoidable. But he who controls his lips and
keeps thoughtful silence is wise. (Prov. 10:19 AMP)

I had never heard the sound before. The loud rumbling seemed to shake the house. It was coming from the basement and I couldn't quite put my finger on what it was. All I knew was that it sounded dangerous. I was tucked cozily in my home office writing, so I put down my coffee mug and ventured downstairs to investigate. However, by the time I reached the basement, the rumbling had stopped. The mystery remained.

A few days later I was in our kitchen. Again the rumblings started. Just as before, I dashed to the basement to try to figure out where the monstrous mechanical noise was coming from. But just like before, the rumbling ceased before I made it to our lower level.

Later that day, I alerted my husband to what had been going on. We weren't sure if it was the furnace, the sump pump, or some other motorized contraption making the reverberating boom. We decided to sit tight and wait for it to happen again.

A few days later, early on a Sunday morning, my husband rose after hitting the "Off" button on his alarm and began to walk down the hallway. He stopped in his tracks when he heard a low but constant humming sound. It was not the loud, shaking boom I had experienced, but nevertheless he dashed to the basement to investigate. There he discovered our septic tank injector was running constantly, its motor clearly approaching burnout.

A quick search on the Internet showed him this was nothing to fool with. We needed to get it repaired immediately. But before we could do that, we needed to shut off the motor, which was now making an even louder, higher pitched hum. He shut off the motor and put a sign on the lower-level bathroom telling our family members not to use it.

Yes, if the motor hadn't been shut down, the consequences could have been extremely messy. Septic and sewer issues must be addressed. If left unattended, they can cause a major stink—literally!

Proverbs 10:19 teaches this is true not only in the plumbing world, but with our mouths as well. As the Amplified Bible version says, "When there are many words, transgression and offense are unavoidable. But he who controls his lips and keeps thoughtful silence is wise."

Have you ever let your constant stream of words get you into trouble? I sure have—more than once. When we constantly run our motormouths, we create a situation with a greater chance of saying something that offends or that we'll later regret. It is nearly unavoidable, as Proverbs 10:19 clearly states. The solution? It's found in the latter half of the verse—we must seek to control our tongues and instead employ the tool of thoughtful silence. Thoughtful silence doesn't mean we never speak; it means we need to zip our lips to avoid uttering something we will later wish we could take back. It means we give careful and prayerful thought to the words we might speak, using discernment to decide if we should speak at all!

Today, let's not just watch what *kind* of words roll off our lips; let's also prudently monitor *how many*. Constantly running motors—whether machine or mouth—are prone to malfunction, thereby causing a mighty mess.

Today's Takeaways

- *Too many words can lead to much heartache.* It's a matter of simple mathematics: the more words we speak, the more opportunities we have to slip up and offend someone—even if the offense is unintentional. An overabundance of rhetoric is often a setup for sin. By intentionally paring back the *quantity* of our words, we can make sure they are *quality* words—true, kind, and necessary.

- *Silence speaks.* Don't underestimate the ability of silence to speak volumes. When we refuse to jump into a conversation full of criticism, gossip, or idle talk, our silence speaks. It attests to our character and indicates to others that we will not be pulled into pettiness. Give your lips a rest and seek to perfect the art of wise and thoughtful silence as advised in today's verse.

Lesson for the Lips

Let's talk quantity. Circle the phrase below that most closely describes you when it comes to how often you talk in social situations or interactions in your relationships:

- I am relatively quiet most of the time, usually speaking less than others in a group setting and rarely voicing my opinion.

- I am quiet sometimes, especially with people I don't know, but other times I talk a great deal in a group setting and offer my opinion when directly asked.

- I talk about as much as the average person, giving my opinions without dominating conversations.

- I am considered by most to be a chatterbox, talking

more than others in almost every social situation and freely giving my opinion.

Based on the description you circled, would you like to make any changes? Do you need to make an adjustment in how often you speak? If so, what? Write out a sentence or two with your goal in this area.

_____

_____

_____

_____

Prayer

*Father, your Word tells me that where there is
a great deal of talk, there is great potential for
offending someone and even sinning. May I
carefully monitor the number of words I speak
today, making sure that my words are true, kind,
and necessary at the moment. Muzzle me when I
need to remain silent. May my words glorify you
and encourage others. In Jesus's name, amen.*

4

ON CHERRY SLUSHIES AND REFRESHING SPRINGS

> No human being can tame the tongue. It is a restless
> evil, full of deadly poison. With the tongue we praise
> our Lord and Father, and with it we curse human beings,
> who have been made in God's likeness. Out of the same
> mouth come praise and cursing. My brothers and sisters,
> this should not be. Can both fresh water and salt water
> flow from the same spring? My brothers and sisters, can
> a fig tree bear olives, or a grapevine bear figs? Neither
> can a salt spring produce fresh water. (James 3:8–12)

My youngest son is a high school football player whose team
just won the state championship—for the fifth time in six
years. GO YELLOW JACKETS! (Total mom brag moment
there.) In addition to lots of excitement for this football family, our past few late summer and fall seasons were filled with

two-a-day practices, early morning weight-lifting sessions, lots of grimy uniforms, and a larger-than-normal grocery bill. Also, as part of my son's and his friends' normal routine, our vehicle made many stops at the local convenience store after practice in the beating sun. There they would grab a slushy iced drink before heading home to shower and crash.

When my son and his friends trek into the store, grab a cup, and place it under a spout on the slushy machine, they have no doubt what will come out of the spigot. If they place it under the spout marked "cherry" and pull, the frosty stream pouring out will indeed be the flavor of that sweet, red fruit. If instead they pull the lever marked "cola," they will receive cola flavor. They needn't worry that a flavor other than what is labeled will come coursing out. (A few of his friends, however, do switch their cups from spout to spout, making a mix of cola, cherry, grape, and lemon-lime. They call this original concoction "Swamp Water"!)

Perhaps we can learn a little lesson from the slushy machine. Each spigot on the device gushes out one type of drink. Our mouths as well should also flow out only one type of speech—namely, that which is refreshing. Today's passage, James 3:8–12, warns, "Out of the same mouth come praise and cursing. My brothers and sisters, this should not be" (v. 10). And the passage starts out with a bold statement: "No human being can tame the tongue." It is restless—even deadly. While the tongue can't be tamed completely, we can seek to temper it.

We may do many good things with our mouths—

encourage the weary, embolden the timid, calm the fretful, or soothe the hurting. We even use our words to praise our heavenly Father. And then at times we turn right around and curse our fellow human beings, who have been made in the image of God. The Bible issues a strong warning against such double-minded speech. Not only should we attempt to correct such conduct because of the warning in Scripture, but we should do it for another reason—because others are watching our behavior.

As Christians, we represent Christ. To represent means to "re-present" him to others. What kind of representation are we if we don't sound at all like the One we are supposed to be "re-presenting"? When our mouths flow forth both praising and cursing, we are not imitating Christ. When we curse our fellow human beings—people who are image bearers of God—we are not advancing the kingdom and pointing others to the gospel message.

Now, before we let ourselves off the hook on this one, we must realize that the type of cursing mentioned here in this passage is not the foul-mouthed, cuss-word slinging type of cursing we often think about. "Curse" in this passage means "to put down or condemn." Certainly this type of speech slips easily into our conversation—sometimes more easily than a cuss word!

So today try to avoid condemnation and put-downs. Watch for double-minded dialogue and speech. Such a mixture is truly like swamp water! Instead, may we strive to utter only praiseworthy words.

Today's Takeaways

- *The tongue cannot be tamed.* This fact is not an excuse for us to chuck any notion of working on our words, nor does it mean we can escape the consequences of bad speech or pay no attention to how we use our language when interacting with others. It means we will never achieve perfection in our speech. We can, however, strive to improve our verbal interactions, which will in turn improve our relationships.

- *When we open our mouths, let's think praise—not put-downs.* Our speech should praise God. Not only is it an honor and a privilege to praise our heavenly Father, but praise should arise naturally as an overflow of a thankful heart. However, in addition to praising God, let's seek to also praise our fellow human beings rather than put them down. May our praise be pure, flowing from hearts that love the image bearers in our lives—both in our families and beyond.

Lesson for the Lips

Let's take the "Praise Over Put-Downs" challenge. In your interactions with others today—whether at home, work, or in your community—seek to utter words of praise and refrain from pronouncing any put-downs. Go out of your way to praise others for the qualities and characteristics you see and appreciate in them. Do not condemn but celebrate. Make it your aim for only praise to stream out of your mouth, and see if it isn't even sweeter and more refreshing than a cherry slushy on a hot summer day!

Prayer

Father, make me mindful today of the way I interact with others. May I praise and not put down. May my words impart grace to others and not show grumpiness. I want to spring forth words of life that refresh the spirit and point others to you. In Jesus's name, amen.

5

WEIGHT CONTROL

The heart of the righteous weighs its answers, but
the mouth of the wicked gushes evil. (Prov. 15:28)

One of my favorite Saturday morning pastimes is going to the
farmer's market. The scene at this huge building filled with
produce and goods from far and near is a delight to the senses.
Colorful fresh-cut flowers. Bright raw veggies. Aromatic fruit.
Handmade soaps and lotions. Woven textiles and dried herbs.
For me, there is no better way to kick off the weekend than to
stroll through the market, soaking in the textures and colors
and smells as I shop.

Whenever I pick apples to make homemade pie, I opt for
the Michigan Northern Spy variety. They are the best for my
family's favorite dessert. "Spies for pies," my mother always
taught me.

When selecting my apples, I make sure to weigh them
on the farmer's old gray metal scale to ensure I have enough

for a pie. (That would be just shy of three pounds per pie, if you must know!)

One by one, I place the apples onto the scale. When I get close to the three-pound mark, I have to choose the perfectly sized apple for the final one, one that will make the dial on the scale read exactly three pounds. It takes a little time, but by carefully weighing, I'm sure to have the perfect number of apples for my tasty pastry.

And so it is with our words. If we want to ensure a pleasant outcome, we need to weigh our words carefully. Especially—as today's challenge verse instructs—when giving someone an answer.

Before we answer children's requests, we must think through what is really best for them before we start to speak. Answering too quickly can lead to a sticky parental situation.

Before we answer a coworker or family member who might be upset with us, we need to consider our response cautiously, selecting phrases that will convey the truth but also promote understanding and peace. Speaking without weighing our words first may escalate the situation, causing an all-out verbal battle.

At times we may be asked a question that needs a gentle and tender response instead of a quick and thoughtless reply. (This is definitely easier said than done!) We need to sort through the options in our minds as we invite the Holy Spirit to give us just the right combination of fruitful words.

If we are to pursue righteousness, we must heed the advice of Proverbs 15:28: "The heart of the righteous weighs its answers."

Notice it says "the heart." It doesn't say the mouth.

Sometimes it's too late to avoid damage by the time the words tumble out of our mouths. When I don't first pause to pray and ponder in my heart, hurtful words may pour out. To avoid causing heartache and even regret, I've learned to contemplate words secretly in my heart, which means running my thoughts through the grid of Scripture before I ever let the words escape from my lips.

Back and forth. Back and forth. Searching for just the right—and righteous—fruitful combination.

Are you ready to carefully weigh your words today? The result will be a delightful offering, pleasing to you, to the hearer, and to God.

It might even be more wonderful than my famous apple pie à la mode!

Today's Takeaways

- *Weigh carefully and measure meticulously.* Weighing and measuring are crucial in so many areas. When you bake a cake from scratch, you must be careful to measure the ingredients. If you don't, your cake may come out dry—or worse yet, create a culinary flop good only for posting on *Pinterest.Fails.* Carpenters know the importance of measuring. Their slogan is "Measure twice. Cut once." They don't want to make a costly mistake, so they give measuring double importance. Weighing our words and measuring our verbal responses are also crucial to ensure a pleasant outcome. Thinking before we speak can prevent us from failing in the area of communication. And it can help to avert a disastrous and costly outcome.

- *Watch your flow.* Proverbs 15:28 states that the mouth of the wicked "gushes evil." When it comes to giving a response, gushing is not good. To gush means "to flow out rapidly and plentifully, often in a sudden stream or burst." When we gush, we have little time to pause and pray. Make it your aim today to slow down the flow of your words from a gush to a trickle. When our words flow in a loving manner and at an appropriate pace, we will avert a damaging flood of feistiness and our relationships will flourish.

Lesson for the Lips

What percent of the time would you say you carefully weigh your words before speaking? Is it closer to 100 percent of the time or closer to . . . well . . . never? Be honest. Write the percentage below.

_____

What are some questions you can learn to ask yourself before giving an answer to someone? Can you think of any helpful phrases to keep in mind that will help you weigh your words? If so, jot them down here:

_____
_____
_____

_____

_____

_____

Prayer

*Father, today I will need to speak many words, both
in person and online. With each interaction comes
the potential for connection and understanding
or for confusion, criticism, and conflict. Help
me weigh my words carefully in my heart before
I ever let them escape my lips. May I watch my
conversational pace and point others to you
with my words. I want the words I utter to bear
much fruit for you. In Jesus's name, amen.*

The Heart-Mind-Mouth Connection

6

SLEEP TALKING AND DAYTIME WORDS

Brothers and sisters, whatever is true, whatever is
noble, whatever is right, whatever is pure, whatever is
lovely, whatever is admirable—if anything is excellent
or praiseworthy—think about such things. (Phil. 4:8)

Have you ever wakened someone from a sound sleep only
to hear them say something off-the-wall? My friend, whose
mom sometimes slept during the day because of late work
hours, has a fond memory of waking her mom to ask her to
sign a permission slip. Her mom's sleepy response? "Please
put my pajamas in the refrigerator."

Now, I'm not poking fun at this mom. I'm sure my kids
have nudged me awake only to hear me make a slew of interesting comments. I merely desire to stress the connection
between our mind and our mouth. Something can happen

in our thoughts—perhaps not even lucid and certainly not yet examined—that can then carry itself all the way out of our mouths through words. Our thoughts are the birthplace of our words. We are constantly processing while we are speaking and while we are listening.

Joseph, the appointed earthly father of Jesus, had plenty to process when he realized Mary was pregnant. The Bible says, "Because Joseph her husband was faithful to the law, and yet did not want to expose her to public disgrace, he had in mind to divorce her quietly" (Matt. 1:19). Joseph had a logical thought path. He took into consideration God's law, but he also considered the shame and hardship his decision to divorce her might cause Mary. He "had in mind" means this idea to divorce her, but quietly, had been formulated and he was ready to take action upon it.

That is, until he received an unexpected visitor. The Bible tells us, "But after he had considered this, an angel of the Lord appeared to him in a dream and said, 'Joseph son of David, do not be afraid to take Mary home as your wife, because what is conceived in her is from the Holy Spirit. She will give birth to a son, and you are to give him the name Jesus, because he will save his people from their sins" (Matt. 1:20–21).

Joseph was asleep when the angel told him these things, but when he awoke, his mind was fixed upon this dream from God. Precisely what was put into Joseph's mind was precisely what happened. Because he realized his dream came from God, Joseph remodeled his response. Today's story teaches us that what's on our mind will affect our actions.

If we take a closer look at the story of Joseph, we see three more pivotal decisions made on the basis of God telling someone something in a dream. In Matthew 2:12, the wise men were warned in a dream not to go back to Herod. In Matthew 2:13, Joseph was told in a dream to leave Egypt. In Matthew 2:19, Joseph was told in a dream to go to Israel.

Now, before you think today's challenge is all about listening to dreams, let me say this: these illustrations show us that what's in our mind will affect our actions. That's clear. Here's what we can't forget, though: *speaking is an action*.

Joseph and the wise men had dreams clearly from God. Sometimes, when we even think we might have a dream with a deeper meaning, we alter our choices. We take it seriously when a thought or plan of action is imposed into our minds from above. But I've been challenged with this question as I've pondered today's topic: *Why are we waiting for God to put something in our minds if he's already had something written for us to put into our minds ourselves?*

We have *all* the divine revelation of the Bible—enough to keep us busy for a lifetime—to memorize and purposefully plant in our thoughts. We don't have to wait. We can impose his words upon our minds now. Right. Now.

Remember that simple illustration of the mom and her sleep talking? She was thinking of something out of her control and talking out of her control as a result. We don't have to live like this. We don't have to talk without thinking. We are alert, alive, aware children of God! We can use this powerful mind-mouth connection to our advantage and to his glory!

Today's Takeaways

- *Exercise your ability to impose.* Consider this verse: "Whatever is true, whatever is noble, whatever is right, whatever is pure, whatever is lovely, whatever is admirable—if anything is excellent or praiseworthy . . ." (Phil. 4:8). Put those things into your mind! Practice imposing Scripture into your thoughts. You have a choice when it comes to what you will think about, so think on good things!

- *Let it flow.* As you work at placing God's Word in your mind, you will find that your speech will change. Maybe you'll talk more. Maybe less. But if you've got good stuff brimming on your tongue, let that good stuff flow! Let all the truth you meditate upon flow fruitfully from your lips. What a sweet sound those words will be!

Lesson for the Lips

Start with Philippians 4:8. This verse is abundantly clear on exactly what should be in our minds, so keep coming back to it to weigh your thoughts and words. In the space below, write Philippians 4:8 as a reminder of what to do for the rest of today. Then circle all the words that tell us what kinds of thoughts we are to have.

_____

_____

_____

_____

_____

_____

Prayer

Dear heavenly Father, I desire to follow you with my mind and my mouth. Allow me to remember that I have the ability, on a daily basis, to make choices about what I put into my mind. On my own I often react with fleshly emotions, muddled thoughts, or angry words. But when my mind is fixed on your truths, I have the ability to answer in a way that pleases you. Thank you for the mind you've given me. Let me use it to honor you. In Jesus's name, amen.

7

YOUR HEART THOUGHTS ARE LOUDER THAN YOU REALIZE

Knowing their thoughts, Jesus said, "Why do you
entertain evil thoughts in your hearts?" (Matt. 9:4)

From the bottom of my heart, I want you to know that God is
teaching me so much through this 40-day challenge, just as I
pray he is teaching you! As I sat down with Matthew 9 today,
it was as if God was using his supernatural neon marker to
highlight some nuggets of truth I had never seen before. Are
you ready for another day of entrusting our words to God and
purposing to glorify him with our speech? I am!

Three unique situations happen consecutively in
Matthew 9. First some men bring a paralyzed friend to Jesus,
and Jesus forgives and heals him. Next Jesus goes to dinner
with tax collectors. And then a woman who suffers from
bleeding approaches Jesus and touches the hem of his cloak.

These stories might be familiar, but let's take a closer look to see in them what God is showing us about our words.

First, in the story of Jesus healing the paralyzed man, we discover that Jesus can hear our unspoken thoughts. Jesus forgave the man of his sins, and "at this, some of the teachers of the law said to themselves, 'This fellow is blaspheming!' Knowing their thoughts, Jesus said, 'Why do you entertain evil thoughts in your hearts?'" (Matt. 9:3–4).

Jesus can hear our thoughts! Not only can he hear our thoughts, but he can *respond* to our thoughts. If Jesus can hear us think, "I hate this," or "I quit," or "I'm not sure I like her very much," with what words do you think Jesus would respond?

When we drill down deeper into Matthew 9:4, we discover the Greek word for *knowing* has several definitions, one of which is "to see with the eyes." So when Jesus "knows our thoughts," he actually *sees* the evil thoughts in our hearts. Whoa.

I sometimes think of my heart and mind as closets. Inside are fresh emotions, percolating questions, and even evil thoughts. The evil thoughts are probably hanging in the back somewhere like an old pink taffeta bridesmaid dress I can't fit into or some hideous fad clothing from the eighties. One thing's for sure: Jesus sees it all and knows what is ill fitting for my waist and for my lips.

Next in Matthew 9 is Jesus's dinner with the tax collectors. Jesus is enjoying food and good conversation. But when the Pharisees spot this shindig, they ask his disciples, "Why does your teacher eat with tax collectors and sinners?" (Matt. 9:11). Notice that the Pharisees didn't direct their question toward Jesus. They asked his disciples. Yet "on hearing this, Jesus said, 'It is not the healthy who need a doctor, but the sick'" (Matt. 9:12).

This exchange reveals another key point for today: Jesus hears our words toward others, and he can respond if he chooses. Why? I believe because every conversation, in some capacity, is directed toward him. We are his children. He loves us. He knows all the hairs on our head, and I believe he also cares about every word spoken from our heart.

Finally, let's look at the woman who touched Jesus's cloak to find healing. The Bible tells us, "A woman who had been subject to bleeding for twelve years came up behind him and touched the edge of his cloak. She said to herself, 'If I only touch his cloak, I will be healed.' Jesus turned and saw her. 'Take heart, daughter,' he said, 'your faith has healed you.' And the woman was healed at that moment" (Matt. 9:20–22).

Jesus even hears the words we speak to ourselves.

Again, we don't know if this woman spoke loudly or softly; we just know she said these things to herself. What a beautiful response Jesus has! He turns and sees her! So I have to ask you this question: *if Jesus were to turn and look at you right now, what would he find you saying to yourself?*

Jesus hears the words of your heart. Jesus hears the words you speak to others. Jesus hears the words you say to yourself.

He sees you and he hears your thoughts. Let's make them faithful today.

Today's Takeaways

- *Keep a clean "word-robe."* Jesus hears those unspoken words of the heart. We talked previously about thoughts being the birthplace for words. Today we likened our heart and mind to a closet. What kind of "word-robe" do you have hanging in there? Keep it clean, fresh, and full of his promises!

- *Consider Jesus's response.* You might not be asking Jesus a question or expecting him to respond when you have a conversation with friends, but he can step in at any time. Consider what he would say to you if he heard your thoughts. Would he see those words and find them to be fitting of the wonderful child of the King that you are?

Lesson for the Lips

Ask God to make you aware of the conversations you have with yourself. I could probably make it a long time without evaluating what I'm actually talking to myself about. What about you? What kinds of conversations do you have with yourself? Write down the unspoken words you tend to repeat to yourself. Then look up one of God's promises that will reorient your unspoken conversation toward something Jesus would find to be sweet. It might look something like this:

- Heart thought: "Ugh, I am so not looking forward to today."

- God thought: "This is the day the LORD has made; We will rejoice and be glad in it" (Ps. 118:24 NKJV).

Prayer

Dear heavenly Father, I need your help in revealing all the contents of my word-robe. You know the thoughts in my heart and mind closet. I want you to see a girl who stores up truth and dwells on your goodness. Allow me to remember what you teach me each day of this challenge. Thank you for your Word and the intimate things you say to me every day. You are a good Father. In Jesus's name, amen.

8

MOUTH-SHUT PRAYERS

When you pray, go into your room, close the door and pray
to your Father, who is unseen. Then your Father, who sees
what is done in secret, will reward you. (Matt. 6:6)

Have you seen the faith-based movie *War Room*? It's a fabulous film about the power of prayer. The lead character reaches out to an older woman, who shares with her the necessity of taking everything before God with focus and strategy. The younger woman then cleans out her closet and turns it into a "prayer closet." Full of Scripture verses and pictures, this place becomes an arena for her to do battle against the enemy.

Our theme verse for today instructs us to go to a private place to pray. It's interesting that we talked about our heart closet yesterday, because today we are considering our prayer closet.

When we imagine a physical prayer closet, we picture a fixed place. Having a space like this is wonderful. It's just too bad we can't take that closet with us. We need a way to take our special spot—our private closet—on the road. You probably know where I'm going with this. Our heart is always the private place we have within us to pray at any time, in any place, and with no audible words at all.

In Genesis 24 we find the account of a man who didn't open his mouth at all, but still managed to say a prayer that made it onto the pages of Scripture.

Abraham was old and needed to settle things before the good Lord called him home, so he called his servant and made him promise to go back to his homeland and find a wife for his son, Isaac. The servant agreed, made the journey, and sat by a well waiting for something divine to happen. In verse 12 he prays, "LORD, God of my master Abraham, make me successful today, and show kindness to my master Abraham." The prayer goes on as the servant asks God to show him the precise woman God would have for Isaac to marry. Then verse 15 says, "Before he had finished praying, Rebekah came out with her jar on her shoulder."

As I'm reading this, I'm thinking it would have been pretty awkward if she had heard the servant praying this aloud: "May it be that when I say to a young woman, 'Please let down your jar that I may have a drink,' and she says, 'Drink, and I'll water your camels too'—let her be the one you have chosen for your servant Isaac" (v. 14).

Have you ever considered how this girl might have responded if she overheard this prayer? She could've taken one look at his bag overflowing with biblical-time valuables, taken another look at the number of camels he had, and then decided that marrying this Isaac fellow would be a fabulous choice. If she'd heard about the special sign of her watering the camels, then she could've just uttered that line and been good to go. If it had happened this way, perhaps we'd be a little less enchanted by the whole interaction.

But it didn't happen like that. She never heard anything he said. Although it seems as if the servant said these words out loud, in verse 45 the whole picture comes into focus. The servant is at dinner with the family when he recounts what happened at the well. In the midst of telling them the details, he says, "Before I finished praying in my heart, Rebekah came out, with her jar on her shoulder" (v. 45).

This servant had prayed the whole thing inside his heart. Mouth shut. No spoken words necessary.

Thinking back to yesterday's challenge and the fact that Jesus can hear the thoughts of our heart, the words we speak to others, and the words we speak to ourselves, we now have a new challenge for today: *Jesus can finish unspoken prayers.*

He not only hears the words we say, but he knows where we're going with them. Jesus knew what the servant was asking for, and he knows what we need before we ask him (Matt. 6:8).

He can finish the silent sentences we speak in our heart closet. Sometimes these mouth-shut prayers are the perfect kind, because the One intended to hear them is the only one who can.

Today's Takeaways

- *Have a physical prayer closet but also use your mobile heart closet.* You will constantly find yourself in situations where a silent prayer is more fitting than anything you might say aloud. On many days it will be more suitable to use a cozy, quiet place to give voice to your prayers. Make use of both types of prayer closets.

- *Let Jesus finish.* "You start praying and I'll finish." Have you ever said that to a friend? What if sometimes we leave space for Jesus to finish the prayer? Maybe he would remind us of another friend to pray for, maybe he'd ask us a question, or best of all, maybe he'd do what he did with Abraham's servant and answer the prayer before we even finished!

Lesson for the Lips

How about we put this idea into practice right now? Write out a prayer below. I'll start, you'll go next, and we'll wait for Jesus to finish. Instead of wrapping up our prayer with our usual closing, I'll leave the prayer open-ended. You can sit for just a few minutes to see how Jesus might finish the prayer.

Prayer

Dear heavenly Father, thank you for this unique lesson from Genesis 24. We have a prayer closet we can take anywhere and use at any time. Remind me that I can always pause and say a silent prayer in my heart closet. Let me trust you, just as this servant trusted you, especially when it comes to the situation most heavy on my heart today. You know what I need to pray. I'll listen and watch as you finish this prayer . . .

9

BUILDING YOUR WORD-ROBE

Moses said to the Lord, "Pardon your servant,
Lord. I have never been eloquent, neither in the
past nor since you have spoken to your servant.
I am slow of speech and tongue." (Ex. 4:10)

Think about your clothes closet for a minute. Is it tidy and
organized or messy and overflowing? How did you end up
with each item you find inside? Did you carefully choose it,
buy it on impulse, or inherit it from someone as a hand-me-
down? When it comes time to organize your closet, how do
you decide whether to keep an item or pass it on to Goodwill?
Sometimes these decisions can be so difficult to make that
one prominent organizational specialist has made millions
of dollars giving advice on what to keep and what to discard,
using one pithy question: "Does it spark joy?"

Thoughts that go into our heart closet are like those
clothes. Sometimes our thoughts are carefully chosen and
sorted. Other times they're rumpled and dirty hand-me-downs

we toss carelessly into the corner. Actually, we make additions to our heart closet much more often than we do our real closet. When we see something on Facebook about a friend, we develop a thought about her. When we goof up and miss a meeting, a thought about ourselves goes into the thought closet. When we read the Bible and soak up the Scriptures, more thoughts are added to this heart closet within us. Then when we verbally (or digitally) respond, something finally comes *out* of the closet. At this moment, it's as if we've made a decision on what we will wear.

If at a job interview you are asked, "What are your strengths and weaknesses?" chances are you already have plenty of items in your word-robe to choose from. For your entire lifetime you've been depositing thoughts—both true and false—and the only response you can choose from in that moment is hanging in your heart closet. There's no buying something new or exchanging an old item. You have to respond right then, and when you do it will be with something you chose to put in there at some earlier point in time.

Moses had to select something worthy from his word-robe when God told him to go speak to Pharaoh. God had already spoken to him in a burning bush, turned his staff into a snake and back, and afflicted his hand with leprosy before healing it. These miraculous acts should have deposited gorgeous thoughts of "God is awesome," "God can do anything," and "God will be with me" into his heart, but instead Moses pulled out this ugly response: "Pardon your servant, Lord. I have never been eloquent, neither in the past nor since you have spoken to your servant. I am slow of speech and tongue" (Ex. 4:10).

Moses selected an unflattering robe he'd been wearing for years with a cut-rate label of "poor speaker." He responded by using thoughts about himself instead of thoughts about God. His heart closet contained so many ill-fitting assumptions that he was unable to quickly don the name-brand truths from his Creator and Designer, Yahweh.

So God responds to Moses by telling him about himself. Not about Moses.

Have you heard the phrase, "Think before you speak"? I believe this is *almost* good advice. We have already been thinking a lot before we speak. The question is, are you thinking a *truthful* thought before you speak? What good is it to think before you speak if your thoughts are shaped by self-deprecating lies or immature frustration?

We must think *truth* before speaking.

Even better, we must think truth about *God*. What we think about God and ourselves is going to be formed a little at a time over a long period of time. Just like our real-life clothes closet contains items from many different seasons (or sizes), our heart closet will contain a word-robe we've created over the course of our whole life. Word-robe building really starts with all the thoughts we buy.

Have you gone shopping lately in the Designer department? Have you had your thoughts tailored by the Master to fit and flatter and shape your unique character? If you had to reach into your heart closet and put on the very best promise of God for one of the biggest responses of your life, what would it be? What kind of promise of God would be hanging in there waiting to be worn?

Today, purpose to put on his promises. They will be sure to spark joy. They will be tailored to your unique personhood. And they will look fabulous on you.

Today's Takeaways

- *Put in only what you want to put on.* We can *put on* only what we've already *put in* our heart closet. We can respond with the falsehoods we've selfishly held on to. Or we can faithfully respond with the promises of God.

- *Plan your purchases.* Just like you are intentional in what you buy for your wardrobe, be strategic in what you allow into your word-robe. Take time now to refresh your heart closet with quality truths that will equip you for today's challenges. What kinds of trials or decisions are you currently in the midst of? Intentionally seek out relevant Scriptures to slide into your heart closet. Then choose to put on a truth tailored to your needs—a truth that will spark joy in your heart.

Lesson for the Lips

Pinning outfits on Pinterest has become an entertaining pastime for many women. There's just something special about putting together the perfect outfit. Consider the perfect combination of promises you'd like to wear today. Draw something creative below or just write a few beautiful, simple truths about God you'd like to clasp around your wrist, fasten to your ear, or wrap softly around your neck.

_____

_____

_____

_____

Prayer

Dear heavenly Father, I can put on only those things
I've already put into my heart closet. I need to make
time on a consistent basis to put truth there. You
had big plans for Moses, and I know you have big
plans for me. I don't want to hold on to lousy labels
that I've been thinking about for much too long. I
surrender them now. Please fill me with promises
about you instead of complaints about myself.
You are the great I AM. In Jesus's name, amen.

10

THIS CONVERSATION TOOK A TURN

An angel of the Lord said to Philip, "Go south to
the road—the desert road—that goes down
from Jerusalem to Gaza." (Acts 8:26)

Have you ever found yourself in a conversation that went
down a road you never anticipated? After getting waist-deep
in words and stuck in statements far from your original topic,
you wondered, "How did we get on this subject?"

Sometimes we simply go off on a tangent, but other
times the Holy Spirit might be driving the conversation right
where it needs to go.

In Acts 8 we have the account of Philip going down an
unplanned road, both in a chariot and in conversation:

An angel of the Lord said to Philip, "Go south to
the road—the desert road—that goes down from

Jerusalem to Gaza." So he started out, and on his way he met an Ethiopian eunuch, an important official in charge of all the treasury of the Kandake (which means "queen of the Ethiopians"). This man had gone to Jerusalem to worship, and on his way home was sitting in his chariot reading the Book of Isaiah the prophet. The Spirit told Philip, "Go to that chariot and stay near it." Then Philip ran up to the chariot and heard the man reading Isaiah the prophet. "Do you understand what you are reading?" Philip asked. "How can I," he said, "unless someone explains it to me?" So he invited Philip to come up and sit with him. (Acts 8:26–31)

This week we've been contemplating the heart, mind, and mouth connection. On this last day, let's also consider the connection between our spirit and our words. Philip initially went down this road because an angel of the Lord told him to. In verse 29 we read that "the Spirit told Philip" to go and join the chariot. We've gleaned numerous truths this week about how Jesus hears our unspoken words, the words we say to others, the words we say to ourselves, and even the power God has to answer our prayers before we've finished praying them! In this passage we can see that God even makes provision ahead of time for words that are not yet spoken. He not only hears words uttered in our hearts, but he also hears the words we've never said at all!

The Ethiopian didn't know he would need someone to interpret the Scriptures for him, but God did. The Ethiopian didn't ask Philip to come on over. God told Philip to do that. God hears questions we might not have even put proper words to in our heart, and he has already prepared for the conversation to happen.

A little further into the story, the Ethiopian asks Philip a specific question about the passage he was reading. Using that opportunity, Philip tells him the good news of Jesus beginning from that very Scripture. Isn't this amazing? God knows about conversations we will have with people we don't even know exist!

If the story ended here, we'd be golden. Philip trusted the Spirit's lead, shared Jesus, and everyone had a nice chariot ride. But the Bible says they traveled even farther down the road. As they went, they came to some water, and the Ethiopian asked to be baptized. When they came out of the water the Spirit of the Lord carried Philip away (Acts 8:36–40).

Philip kept going down that conversational road until the Spirit took him off that road. We can't settle for sharing Jesus and then stopping; God may have salvation waiting just a little further down that conversational path. How wise we will be to continue listening and engaging until the Spirit has finished his work.

The last phrase that stands out to me from this story is "the desert road." God told Philip to go down a road that was a *desert* road. This I know for sure: sometimes dry conversations will lead someone down a path to Living Water. Don't balk at conversations that seem empty; it could be God is sending you to quench another's soul.

Go down the conversational roads God would have you go down. Travel a little while. You could be the provision for a thirsty soul. God could be sending you to answer questions about Jesus just about to be asked.

He hears the salvation song coming from hearts that are soon to be his.

Today's Takeaways

- *Don't judge a conversation by its beginning.* You don't know where a conversation will lead. Allow a firm connection between the Holy Spirit and your words so he can guide each conversation toward Jesus and to a place of fruitfulness. Even if a conversation starts dry, let it end full of the Living Water that flows from inside us (John 7:38).

- *Keep going.* Don't stop at sharing Jesus with someone. Travel through the exchange as far as the Holy Spirit will take you both. Be sensitive to not say more or less than necessary. There is no need for you to press. You need only to be gentle, obedient, and truthful.

Lesson for the Lips

The next time you're in a conversation that seems dry, stay a little longer and ask the Holy Spirit to guide you. You may be afforded the opportunity to speak some Scripture. You may have the opportunity to listen a little longer. Either way, may God guide you.

Prayer

Dear heavenly Father, thank you for the obedience of Philip. Thank you for these remarkable truths. You provide answers to questions we didn't know we'd have. You also provide salvation for us even before we are able to understand it. Bless our upcoming conversations and let them lead straight to you. In Jesus's name, amen.

Oh, the Places You Go (and the Things You Say)

11

R-E-S-P-E-C-T

Respect everyone, and love the family of believers.
Fear God, and respect the king. (1 Peter 2:17 NLT)

It was a rainy winter afternoon. Our youngest son was in middle school and I was walking down the school hallway following a meeting. As I opened my umbrella to ward off the chilly shower, I heard a woman's voice pipe up. "Hello? Excuse me. May I ask you a question?"

I turned to see one of the lunchroom workers. "Are you Spencer's mother?" she inquired, adjusting her hairnet.

"Yes," I answered. "Is something wrong?" My heart fluttered and fretted. I had just left the vice principal's office, where my son sat busted for pulling a stunt in class—one he and his friends found completely hysterical but the substitute teacher saw no humor in. I was not bursting with parental pride. Now I feared he'd also misbehaved in the lunchroom.

"Oh, no. Nothing is wrong at all!" she asserted. "I just wanted to tell you how respectful your son is. He never fails to ask if I'm having a good day or flash a huge smile and thank me when I hand him his food. And he addresses me as 'ma'am' and calls the custodian 'sir.' Such a fine and respectful son you've raised!"

To say that her words thrilled this parent's heart would be an understatement. In fact, it was a little kiss from God that day when this thoughtful school employee pointed out a positive quality she saw in my teenage son's behavior.

Respect is frequently absent in our society. In person—and especially online—snark and sarcasm often rule. Talking down to someone or insulting one another is the new norm. For adults and for kids, respect is often nowhere to be found.

No longer do we use terms like "sir" and "ma'am" when speaking to a stranger. Addressing elders with terms of esteem is rare as well. And having respect for authority seems to have gone out of style long ago.

Today's digital world has taken this to a new level. It has become commonplace to sling opinions on a screen, whether on social media or while leaving a comment on a blog post. And unfortunately, sometimes these comments and thoughts aren't tucked in an envelope of respect. Instead they are laced with cynicism, mockery, or disdain.

However, today's challenge verse talks about respect. And not just respecting those in authority, like a teacher, a police officer, or a judge. It goes so far as to say that we are to respect everyone.

Everyone.

Does this mean the grumpy neighbor whose dog uses your yard as an outhouse? Yes.

Does it include your combative relative who never speaks respectfully to you? Yes.

What about the difficult person on that committee with you, whose personality and behavior get on your very last nerve? Yep. That one too.

We can learn to speak respectfully no matter the situation. By drawing on the power of the Holy Spirit to temper our tongues and help us weigh our words, we can speak in a polite tone. This doesn't mean we don't speak the truth. It just means we verbalize it in an honorable and honoring way.

We can reflect the love of Jesus when we engage in conversations with a calm, collected, and civil tone.

Then others might notice—as in the case of the lunchroom lady and my prank-pulling son—that our speech isn't snappy, impolite, or rude. Our language is respectful. Our words are honoring—to those we are talking to and, more importantly, to God.

Today's Takeaways

- *Respecting others shows our fear of God.* I used to read the phrase "fear God" and get confused. What does it mean to fear God? Isn't God love? If so, why should we be scared of him? But in Scripture, fearing God has more to do with being in awe of him, reverencing him, and respecting him. And since humans have been made in God's likeness and bear his image, when we respect others with our words and actions, we are also reverencing God.

- *Everyone means everyone.* We can't miss the point in this Scripture. We are to respect everyone, not just those we like. Not just those who are easy to get along with. A mark of true Christians is that they do not play favorites. Luke 6:32 states, "If you love those who love you, what credit is that to you? Even sinners love those who love them." Our behavior should stand out. It stands out when we choose to show honor and respect to everyone, regardless of who they are or what we think of them.

Lesson for the Lips

Can you name someone in your life who speaks respectfully a majority of the time? What stands out the most to you about how that person uses his or her words?

Do you know someone you have a hard time speaking to respectfully? Why do you think you have trouble showing that person respect with your speech?

Challenge: Think about the person you just named. It's been said if we look hard enough, we can find a good quality in anyone. So name one good quality about this person. Take your time . . . you'll eventually find something. Write it here:

_____

_____

Okay . . . *deep breath* . . . reach out to that person with your words this week—either spoken, written, texted, or typed—and say you admire that quality in them. Do not expect a response. Do it only to show love and display respect. As you do, think about this verse: Romans 12:10, "Love each other with genuine affection, and take delight in honoring each other" (NLT).

Prayer

Father, help me think before I speak, making sure my words are respectful. Let my tone be tempered and my manner kind. I want to please you and honor others with my speech. In Jesus's name, amen.

12

THAT TIME I SPIED UGLY IN THE MIRROR

Love must be sincere. Hate what is evil; cling to what is good. Be devoted to one another in love. Honor one another above yourselves. Never be lacking in zeal, but keep your spiritual fervor, serving the Lord. (Rom. 12:9–11)

I'll never forget the day I saw myself in that mirror. Even though over a decade of time has passed since I caught the glimpse, the image is still vivid. And I'm sorry to say it wasn't a pretty one.

My then six-year-old daughter and her three-year-old brother were playing together in their bedroom. I strolled down the hall to check on the baby, who was due up from his nap soon. As I approached the room where the kids were playing, I heard Mackenzie's voice pipe up as she expressed to Mitchell her immense displeasure. You see, he wasn't stacking the plastic blocks in a manner that suited her. As I neared the door I heard her sharply declare, "No, Mitchell. Not that way! Oh, just give it to me! Anybody with a brain knows they go like this, not like that. Can't you ever do anything right?" Her words, though unkind, weren't the real issue. What bothered me most was my daughter's caustic, condescending tone. And I was not going to let her get away with it.

I stepped into the room and with classic mom form—hand on hip, finger pointed, throwing the child's middle name in for emphasis—I gave it to her. "Mackenzie Leith Ehman! Young lady, I don't ever want to hear you talk like that to your brother again!"

Without even looking up from her pile of blocks, she quickly and calmly retorted, "Why not, Mama? You talk like that to Daddy all the time."

It was then that I saw it. The ugly in the mirror.

Ouch!

My kids often serve as a painfully honest mirror when it comes to my attitudes and actions. The offense my daughter had committed that day paled in comparison to the disrespectful way I had treated my husband many times before. I cried and prayed and cried some more. I told my husband what had transpired. I then told my Bible study group, which comprised other moms. Turns out I wasn't the only mom who had a little mirror in her house. Many of us had seen ourselves vividly reflected through the voices and actions of our offspring. We vowed together to keep our words and tones in check. Of course, we found out this is often easier said than done.

Today's challenge verse talks about hating what is evil,

clinging to what is good, and honoring one another above ourselves. When I talked to my husband in a disrespectful tone, I certainly was not keeping my speech in line with the directives in this verse. And sadly, my bad behavior had served as a poor example for my daughter, who then began to mimic what she saw. I knew something had to change.

It's been a long time since I spied my ugly self in the mirror that day. I still struggle at times with a sharp tongue, often saying things "in jest" that in reality are unkind. And my kids now reserve the right to call me on the carpet for such behavior. We moms need to remind ourselves that little and not-so-little eyes are watching, and in many cases imitating what they see. What's in your mirror?

Today's Takeaways

- *Mimic an evil-hating, good-clinging, sincerely loving person.* Name a person you know who gets a good grade in the subjects spelled out in Romans 12:9–10 (loves sincerely, hates evil, clings to good, shows honor). What is different about him or her—especially when it comes to speech? What do they do and not do that makes them a good example of a person who lives out the instructions in this passage?

- *Set a recorder.* Pay close attention to your words and tone this week as you interact with your husband or others you are close to. What would you see if you were videotaped and then had to watch a playback of how you speak to them? Would others be able to tell from your encounters that you respect your spouse, boss, coworkers, or customers?

Lesson for the Lips

Ask yourself, "Who could hold me accountable in the area of speaking respectfully?" Choose someone who will be honest with you and cares enough about you to tell you the truth and point you to God. Contact that person to see if he or she is willing to check in with you periodically to inquire how you are doing.

For the married, brave at heart parent only: Ask your children to be honest with you. Question them about what they observe when you speak to your spouse. Is there anything they think you should clean up? What grade would they give you when it comes to how you treat your husband? Tell them you're trying to obey the Bible by respecting and honoring him, and you just need a little report card from them to know how you are doing and to enable you to make the necessary changes.

Meditate on this verse today to help you in your quest to speak with honor to others: "Do not let any unwholesome talk come out of your mouths, but only what is helpful for building others up according to their needs, that it may benefit those who listen" (Eph. 4:29).

Prayer

Dear Lord, forgive me for the times I have used my words, attitudes, and actions as weapons of disrespect toward another person. Empower and enable me to live a life that accurately reflects the type of behavior that loves sincerely, clings to what is good, and hates evil. In Jesus's name, amen.

13

WHEN YOU'RE ABOUT TO CROSS THE LINE

When tempted, no one should say, "God is tempting me."
For God cannot be tempted by evil, nor does he tempt
anyone; but each person is tempted when they are dragged
away by their own evil desire and enticed. Then, after
desire has conceived, it gives birth to sin; and sin, when
it is full-grown, gives birth to death. (James 1:13–15)

Impossible! How can this be? Why, I'm certain I never crossed the line!"

Out tumbled the words from my disbelieving mouth during a recent trip with my family to a neighboring state. My husband and I stood staring at the two left-wheel wells on our family minivan that now sat spattered with bright yellow paint. While driving through construction in a congested metropolitan area, I had traveled a little too close to the freshly painted neon line that separates two-way traffic.

While I was keenly aware the workers had just finished placing the sunny stripes on the pitch-black pavement, I was sure I had driven in a manner that, although closely hugging the lines, had not crossed them. Much to my dismay, when the van's tires rolled to a halt at a rest stop, the truth was revealed: Had I crossed the line? No, I hadn't. There was no paint on the tires. However, my getting ever-so-close was enough to cause the wet paint to spatter and stick itself stubbornly to my vehicle's wheel wells, resulting in a public display of my too-close behavior.

Sometimes we do the same thing with sin—especially sins of speech. Oh, we make sure we don't cross the line, but we skirt dangerously close to it. We toy with temptation. We wink at seduction. We let bad behavior beckon us.

Perhaps we say just enough that it borders on gossip and gets our point across while technically remaining innocent. Maybe we speak about someone in a veiled, cryptic way that doesn't actually demean them, but paints an unflattering picture of them nonetheless. How about "innocent" but bantering relationships forged with members of the opposite sex, which could lead to a dangerous and tempting situation? Do we reason and reckon that some of these verbal behaviors aren't "that bad," but in reality they come so close to the line that they drag us away from God? And once the dragging starts, we're hooked. Then we might find ourselves standing in a very public way with sin spattered all over us.

Instead of asking ourselves how close we can get to the line, perhaps the opposite approach is best. We must remind ourselves how desperately near we must stay to the Lord Jesus. So near that wandering even slightly away feels foreign, unfamiliar. So near that we instantly recognize temptation is happening and petition God for strength to resist it. Let's vow together to stick safely by our Savior and a world away from that nasty line of sin.

Today's Takeaways

- *Sin spatters.* Just as I didn't have to touch any paint for it to appear on the side of our vehicle, sometimes we don't have to partake in sin for it to affect us. Just flirting with it, pondering doing it, or getting close to the line causes hurt and heartache. Sin is like fire—it can cause damage from not only the flame but also from the smoke and the heat. Flirting with the Devil never ends well. So remember that sin spatters and stay far away from its reach.

- *Paint removal is tough and tedious.* Attempting to remove that neon yellow paint from our steel-gray minivan was tough and tedious. We had to scrub long and hard. Likewise, the ramifications of our sinful speech can be tough to erase. Feelings get hurt. Relationships are damaged. While forgiveness can occur, it is a painstaking process. Better not to speak words of sin in the first place than to have to clean up the mess left in their wake.

Lesson for the Lips

Have you been cutting it a bit too close to the line in an area of your speech? Have your words bordered on gossip? Has your speech painted your spouse in a negative light, if even in a humorous and kidding way? Has your tone been disrespectful to your boss or coworker? Take a moment to ponder this in prayer. Then write down any area that comes to mind.

How can the story of my cutting it too close to the line while driving help you resist the temptation to sin with your words today? What practical actions can keep you from coming too close to crossing the line of sin in your life? Try to commit one of the following verses to memory to help in your quest to not give in to temptation:

- 1 Corinthians 10:13: "No temptation has overtaken you except what is common to mankind. And God is faithful; he will not let you be tempted beyond what you can bear. But when you are tempted, he will also provide a way out so that you can endure it."

- Psalm 119:10–11 (AMPC): "With my whole heart have I sought You, inquiring for and of You and yearning for You; Oh, let me not wander or step aside [either in ignorance or willfully] from Your commandments. Your word have I laid up in my heart, that I might not sin against You."

Prayer

Dear Lord, prick my heart when I begin to veer from your perfect path and wander dangerously close to the line of sin. At those times, may I obey your commanding voice, however still and small it may be, and rush back safely to your side. In Jesus's name, amen.

14

WHEN FACEBOOK MAKES YOU FEISTY

You are still worldly. For since there is jealousy and
quarreling among you, are you not worldly? Are
you not acting like mere humans? (1 Cor. 3:3)

I sat in the waiting room of the dentist's office, scrolling through the feed on my cell phone. Perhaps reading a few articles would help me forget about the needles and numbing I was about to receive when my tooth got a new crown. And so I perused the various links I saw, occasionally clicking on one to read it.

One title caught my eye. It was an article about how Facebook can make you jealous. What in the world? That concept was rather foreign to me. Up until that time, Facebook to me was just a place to connect with old friends, a spot for people to post pictures and random facts about their lives—like what they ate for lunch. I didn't see it as a breeding ground for jealousy.

The article started off talking about how we escape our real lives each day, going to a virtual vacation destination: Facebook. The rest of the article unpacked reasons Facebook can trigger feelings of envy and jealousy in us. And so I started to think about my own experience with this mode of social media to see if that was true, and I have to say it is!

I have seen in the lives of teenagers how jealousy rears its ugly head. When I was a teen, if I didn't get invited to a slumber party, I might hear other girls discussing it the following Monday in the lunchroom, but I didn't have to watch it unfold in real time right before my eyes on social media. And it isn't just teenage girls who struggle with feelings of envy while they stare at their phone or computer screen. I have seen adult friends of mine become jealous when they spied the wonderful Valentine gift another woman received from her husband while their own spouse forgot what day it even was. Personally, I have struggled with feelings of jealousy when a friend posted about the academic success of her child at a time when one of my sons dealt with a learning disability. Or I've envied vacation pictures during a year our family couldn't afford to take one.

But it doesn't stop with jealousy or envy. The online culture of freely typed words also leads to quarrels. Fights break out in comment threads. Arguments abound and opinions fly. While social media can certainly be used for good—to ask for prayer or spread happy news—it certainly can deteriorate quickly.

The verse we are focusing on today talks about jealousy and quarreling, characterizing such behavior as worldly. We are behaving as sinful humans when we display words and actions such as these, rather than behaving in a manner that reflects Christ. While that seems to be an obvious point of this verse, I began to wonder what the relationship was between jealousy and quarreling. Do feelings of jealousy lead to words of fighting? I think sometimes they do.

When we become jealous of someone, it is easy to let feelings of hate creep in. When we begin to loathe, sometimes we lash out. Perhaps we type some words of sarcasm. Or maybe the feelings of jealousy triggered by something we see online leads us to gossip about that person with one of our friends. Worldly behavior can lead to rotten words. We must not allow worldly behavior—namely, jealousy and quarreling—to corrupt our relationships with others. Instead we must seek to behave maturely, not let ourselves act like an immature junior higher.

Let's vow this week to use social media properly and not allow it to trigger wrong behavior in us or tempt us to use our words wickedly.

Today's Takeaways

- *Leave it behind.* One word in today's challenge verse pops out at me: *still.* "You are *still* worldly." This denotes the fact that jealous and quarrelsome behavior is something we did before we met Christ. It is baggage we are tempted to carry into our current relationships. But it doesn't belong there. We were worldly before our hearts were made new. Exchanging our old behavior for new and godly thought patterns and actions isn't the easiest thing to do, but it should be our aim. Let's be mindful of this manner of behaving and leave it in our past where it belongs.

- *Walk away.* If being on social media is a trigger for jealousy, or a place where you find yourself quarreling, walk away. Perhaps it is time you went on a Facebook fast. Or vowed to stay off Twitter for a month. Sometimes we need a complete break from whatever is tempting us to behave in a worldly manner. Then we can start over again with new boundaries in place. Two different Junes in a row I took a month-long Facebook fast. Upon returning, I not only noticed I logged onto Facebook less frequently, but I wasn't so drawn into what was happening with others in a comparing sort of way.

Lesson for the Lips

Have you ever found yourself jealous when you saw something on social media? Have those feelings of jealousy led to combativeness or quarreling? If so, how?

On a scale of 1 to 10, how would you rank yourself when it comes to online quarrels you see in comment threads or on Twitter or Facebook feeds? Let's say the number 1 represents

"I never participate in online quarrels" and 10 stands for "I love a good online fight and often jump in and give my opinion." Be honest. Write the number below.

_____

How would you like to see that number change? What can you do to bring about that change? Write a goal for yourself in this area.

_____
_____
_____
_____

Prayer

Father, sometimes it's hard for me to watch my words while I'm online. Help me to be content with the life you have given me and not be jealous of others. Prevent me from getting caught up in quarrels, because I know they prove only one thing—that I am still worldly. I want my words online to point others to you and the good news of redemption. In Jesus's name, amen.

15

FOLLOWING FROM AFAR

Peter followed him at a distance, right up to the
courtyard of the high priest. He entered and sat down
with the guards to see the outcome. (Matt. 26:58)

I sat in the sanctuary all alone, hot tears trickling down my
young face. As a high school senior, I often attended our
church's open-door, self-serve communion time held a few
days each year. The church was left unlocked, providing a
place to be alone with God, to pray or read the Bible. Then
the elements were at the altar. When ready, believers could
partake of the bread and the cup. Although I had done this
many times, that night would forever be seared in my mind.

I'd been a follower of Christ for just over a year, having
first dedicated my life to him at a youth retreat. The next
twelve months, though an exciting time of growth, were also
filled with sorrow. I lost friends. I no longer fit with the "in"
crowd. I had no desire to attend certain parties I knew God

wouldn't approve of or engage in conversations I wouldn't want him to hear.

So I clung to my crisp new Bible and rushed home each afternoon, eager to read more and make notations in the margins. My youth group and my mentor—a pastor's wife and mom of two—became my lifelines. I desperately wanted to know how to live this new Christian life in a way that made Jesus proud.

But as I sat there that night, I felt as if I had failed God. The popular kids at school had shut me out, so I was grateful when a new group of kids took me in. But things were beginning to get sticky there too. They were challenging my faith, asking questions, eloquently arguing against the existence of God. So normally chatty me went silent. I knew I should say something, but I remained painfully wordless. My silence spoke volumes and, in a way, denied Christ.

That day, as I sat alone in my church crying and searching my soul, I read today's challenge verse. The words stung. "Peter followed him at a distance . . ." (Matt. 26:58 NIV). That was me! I followed my sweet Jesus, but often at a distance, not wanting to get too close, to be lumped in with the Bible-thumping fanatics, to be labeled a "Jesus freak." That night was a wake-up call. I didn't want to lurk in the shadows any longer. I wanted to be so closely associated with Jesus that I cared not what any soul on earth thought. I left with a renewed commitment to this goal.

In his mercy, God allowed me to come across many more verses about Peter in the next few weeks as I flung myself on my bed and opened my Bible each afternoon after school.

I witnessed his three-time denial. Then I saw his sorrow, his repentance, his eventual boldness for Christ. I garnered encouragement from knowing that this once-hesitant, in-the-shadows disciple became a bold, world-changing servant of God. And just weeks later, our youth group took a personality test that matches you with a biblical character. My result came back as—you guessed it—Peter! I knew then that if he could learn to follow boldly, then I could too.

Oh, may God help us all to turn our fear of associating with him into boldness for his kingdom! The world is waiting and watching. Will we pursue him closely or follow at a distance?

Today's Takeaways

- *Assess your public witness.* Often, we frequently talk about our personal, private walk with Jesus but seldom discuss our public walk—how overt we are when it comes to sharing our faith. Often we let peer pressure or societal expectations silence us, or perhaps we go to the opposite extreme, sharing aggressively without regard to how our message is being received. Walking close to Jesus will help us avoid both extremes, for he will nudge us when to speak up and point out when a more subtle approach is needed.

- *Be yourself and listen to the Spirit.* Not everyone is called to public ministry, but all Christians are called to respond to seekers and questioners, giving them an account for the hope they have. Depending on your personality, with whom you are communicating, and what the situation is, you might choose to share your personal story of how you came to know Christ and what he means to you, share a relevant Bible verse or truth from Scripture, or point out a Christian book that addresses the person's question. The possibilities are endless. Just be yourself and listen to the Spirit; he will guide you on what to do or what to say.

Lesson for the Lips

Ponder—and perhaps even memorize—one of the following portions of Scripture to help you speak up for Christ without fear:

- 1 Peter 3:14–16: "'Do not fear their threats; do not be frightened.' But in your hearts revere Christ as Lord. Always be prepared to give an answer to everyone who asks you to give the reason for the hope that you have. But do this with gentleness and respect, keeping a clear conscience, so that those who speak maliciously against your good behavior in Christ may be ashamed of their slander."

- Psalm 40:8–10: "I desire to do your will, my God; your law is within my heart. I proclaim your saving acts in the great assembly; I do not seal my lips,

Lord, as you know. I do not hide your righteousness in my heart; I speak of your faithfulness and your saving help. I do not conceal your love and your faithfulness from the great assembly."

Prayer

Dear Lord, may I not shirk from associating myself closely with you by what I say for all the world to hear. I want to reflect you, not reject you. Please grant me the courage to do so. In Jesus's name, amen.

Taming Our Tempers

16

ONE-BULLET BARNEY

Whoever restrains his words has knowledge, and he who has
a cool spirit is a man of understanding. (Prov. 17:27 ESV)

When I was a little girl, one of my favorite places to pass
the time was on our couch, snuggled up on my father's lap,
watching television. One of my dad's most-loved programs
was also one of mine—*The Andy Griffith Show*. The plot
centered around the folk of a small town called Mayberry
and featured Sheriff Andy Taylor, a widower, his precocious
young son, Opie, and their loving Aunt Bee who kept everything together on the home front. But my favorite character of
all was the sheriff's bumbling sidekick, Deputy Barney Fife. I
laughed my way through Barney's antics.

Trigger-happy Barney prided himself on being "quick to
the draw," and he loved to "watch the lead fly." He would frantically grab for his gun whenever there was any semblance of
trouble brewing. In haste and excited recklessness, he would
try to draw his pistol from his holster to protect the town from

evil, but in doing so, he'd shoot from the hip and almost shoot himself in the foot.

Now, before we get lost in idioms and Mayberry reminiscing, let's make a practical application. We might not carry a deputy's pistol, but we shouldn't shoot from the hip with our words either. Better said, we shouldn't "shoot from the lip."

Today's verse, our challenge from the book of Proverbs, states, "Whoever restrains his words has knowledge, and he who has a cool spirit is a man of understanding" (17:27 ESV). The book of Proverbs has many pieces of advice for how and how not to use our words. In fact, just a few pages later in Proverbs 29:20 we read, "Do you see a man who is hasty in his words? There is more hope for a fool than for him" (ESV).

When I'm hasty with my words, I end up shooting myself in the foot, just as Barney almost did with his pistol, literally. It's foolish, and in my own reality apart from TV land, shooting from the lip doesn't hurt just me. I also wound innocent bystanders on the other end of my unfortunate misfire, causing damage when my words tear into another's heart.

So how do we remedy this quick-to-the-draw impulse and keep ourselves from the damaging habit of shooting from the lip?

We need to do what Proverbs 17:27 urges: restrain our words and have knowledge and a cool spirit. This means to stop, really think about what to say, and allow our emotions to simmer down a bit before we let any words emerge from our mouth.

Back in Mayberry, the insightful Sheriff Taylor required Deputy Fife to keep his only bullet tucked safely in his shirt pocket. This way it took Barney a few seconds to load his gun, giving him time to think before he acted. When ol' One-Bullet Barney listened to his boss's order, he had fewer accidents and less embarrassment.

However, Barney didn't always take Andy's advice. Throughout the episodes, the gawky deputy periodically reverted to old habits and prematurely loaded his gun. Those instances resulted in plenty of laughs, but they also serve as reminders that we can easily slip into our old "quick-draw" selves.

Barney had to make a choice to keep his bullet in his pocket. We have to make the choice every day to put away the verbal ammunition and restrain our words. When we choose to pause and ponder before we let words fly, we can keep a misfire from occurring.

Can we put our words away? Can we tuck them safely in a place where we will have to stop, think, and cool down before speaking? Let's keep our speech unlocked and unloaded, and not make it a practice to mindlessly shoot from the lip.

Today's Takeaways

- *Restraining is tied to knowledge.* When we think of knowledge, we may picture someone who has lots of information and is readily able to share it at any moment. But our verse today talks about knowledge in a different way. It tells us someone who has knowledge may hold back from what they would like to say. Having control and restraining our words means we are smart indeed. Ponder this thought: be smart—be silent! When we are silent we don't have to worry about regrets from angry words we've let fly. Let's save ourselves some regret today.

- *Take your temperature.* If you were to take the temperature on your spirit, would you say it is cool? Lukewarm? Burning hot? In the original Hebrew of this text in Proverbs 17:27, a cool spirit means one that is calm, sedate, and not easily provoked. Is that how you would describe your spirit today?

Lesson for the Lips

James 1:19 reads, "Know this, my beloved brothers: let every person be quick to hear, slow to speak, slow to anger" (ESV).

On a scale of 1 to 10 (with 1 being "almost never" and 10 being "practically always"), how often do you ponder what you will say before you open your mouth? Record that number here in the space provided.

If you would like to see that number change for the better, what is one action step you could take today to make it happen?

Prayer

Father, help me pause and ponder before I speak, preventing myself from thoughtlessly shooting from the lip. May I be wise, restraining my words when necessary. Grant me a cool and calm spirit. I want my words to please you and not wound others. In Jesus's name, amen.

17

A SPRINKLE OF SALT

Be wise in the way you act toward outsiders; make the
most of every opportunity. Let your conversation be
always full of grace, seasoned with salt, so that you
may know how to answer everyone. (Col. 4:5–6)

Whenever you sit down to dine—whether at home or in a
restaurant—what is usually on the table, ready to be added
to your dish, should you desire to spice it up a bit? Salt. On
the periodic table of elements it is named sodium chloride—
NaCl. Salt is the number one flavor enhancer in the world.

Over a quarter billion pounds of salt are produced each
year. Diners put a dash of it on their casseroles, sprinkle it on
piping hot potatoes, and add a pinch or two to a bowl of soup.
Salt is even added to sweet things to intensify their sweetness.
My father always puts it on his slices of melon. The barista at
my local coffeehouse cracks some sea salt on top of caramel
hot cocoa and its mounds of whipped cream. And have you
ever tasted dark chocolate with sea salt? Oh. My. Word.

Most traditional baked dessert recipes include salt. One time I forgot to add salt to a mint brownie recipe. When I tasted it I could tell something was wrong. There was plenty of mint and cocoa powder, the two main flavors of the dish, but somehow it didn't taste right. Even though the recipe called for only half a teaspoon of salt, omitting it ruined the normally delicious treat. It takes only a little salt to coax out the wonderful flavors around it.

When we are told our speech should be seasoned with salt, perhaps it means we should ask ourselves if we are bringing out sweetness in both our choice of words and in our conversation with others, especially in online conversations. Are we sprinkling on the flavor of Christ or adding not just bland but maybe even *bad* ingredients? Do our words add flavor?

This concept of having salty speech has always intrigued me. In high school, my pastor gave a message series on the Sermon on the Mount. At one point Jesus states, "You are the salt of the earth. But if the salt loses its saltiness, how can it be made salty again? It is no longer good for anything, except to be thrown out and trampled underfoot" (Matt. 5:13). My minister devoted an entire message to explaining what being "the salt of the earth" meant. I had never considered the many uses of salt, especially in the ancient world of Jesus's day. So when I did a little research, I discovered even more about the many uses and the significance of salt. It doesn't only have to do with adding flavor.

Here are some other uses of salt and corresponding questions we can ask ourselves about seasoning our speech with salt:

Salt preserves. Do our words preserve God's Word? Are

we accurately reflecting his thoughts and heart in the phrases we speak? Are we helping to improve a situation and avoid decay?

Salt adds value. Do our words add value to the conversation at hand or are they empty and worthless?

Salt purifies and softens. Are the words we utter pure and truthful? Are they soft and kind or harsh and hostile?

Salt melts hard ice. Do we phrase our speech in such a way as to help to melt an icy conversation and bring out the best in others? Do we seek to cover offenses and smooth rough situations?

Salt prevents infection in a wound. When an interaction starts to turn ugly—either between us and another person or in a group situation—do our words try to help heal, preventing further toxicity from spreading?

It's also important to note that too much salt ruins "the soup." While we are called to season our speech with salt, we must know how to keep it clear and concise. Too much salt will not only spoil the soup but can overpower a conversation as well.

So many uses for—and some warnings about—salt. So many applications for our speech!

Today's Takeaways

- *Be wise—maximize!* The first sentence of today's portion of Scripture urges, "Be wise in the way you act toward outsiders; make the most of every opportunity." There is wisdom in maximizing our conversations with others. We would do well to use our conversations to impart the most good we can, not interacting in a haphazard or careless manner but with keen perception.

- *Embrace grace.* In urging us to season our speech with salt, Colossians also tells us to fill our conversations with grace. The word *grace* in the New Testament means being kind, winning with pleasantness, and doing what makes one's words attractive. Think of your speech as sprinkling kindness wherever you go. What a contrast to so many conversations we witness today that are laced with snark and callousness. Make gracious speech your aim.

Lesson for the Lips

Colossians 4:6 mentions salty speech directly in reference to knowing "how to answer everyone." Can you think of a time when you gave an answer to someone and it did not go well? Briefly describe it here in the space provided:

_____

_____

_____

_____

Now look back over the list of salt's various uses. Which one could you have employed to change how you gave your answer for the better? If you could go back in time, how would you answer differently based on that particular quality of salt?

Prayer

Father, may I be ever mindful of just what I am sprinkling on a conversation when I use my words. Help my speech be seasoned with salt so I will know how to answer everyone. I want my words to preserve, soften and purify, add value, melt the tension of difficult situations, and stop the spread of pain and hurt. Please grant me salty speech. In Jesus's name, amen.

18

LACED WITH GRACE

Gracious words are a honeycomb, sweet to the
soul and healing to the bones. (Prov. 16:24)

I am such a Bible nerd. Not only do I love to learn the meaning behind the Hebrew or Greek words in Scripture, but I like to study certain English words that pop up at me, pogo-stick style, to find out why a particular word or phrase is used. And so I grew curious one day. *Why does God use a honeycomb to describe gracious, sweet, and healing speech?* I didn't have to look far for my answer.

Jake is a teenage boy who lives in our neighborhood. He's an outstanding football player and a wrestler. He's also a beekeeper who sells his amber jars of honey at local festivals and fairs. I decided to interview this high school entrepreneur one afternoon to discover all I could about the honey-making biz.

Jake told me the flavor and intensity of honey depends on what kind of nectar the bees drink in. Clover nectar produces honey that is light and heavenly sweet. Another flower's nectar might create a dark, bitter product, with a lingering, unpleasant aftertaste. Smart beekeepers ensure that a beehive is strategically placed near a large patch of clover if they want to sell the sweetest, most delectable honey.

Jake also told me how crucial it is that the beehive be placed where the sun will hit it first thing in the morning, warming up the bees and causing them to get to work churning out the greatest quantity of sweet syrup possible.

"So," I questioned my young friend, "is it safe to say the sweetness or bitterness of honey is determined by what the bee drinks in and the amount of time it spends in the sun—especially early in the morning?"

"Exactly!" he replied.

DING! DING! DING! We have a winner. I think I found my answer. *Perhaps it is also true that the sweetness or bitterness of our words will be determined by what we drink in and the amount of time we spend early with the Son.*

But choosing grace will sometimes cost us. Spats and squabbles are oh-so-easy to fall into. We will have to resist the urge to lash out in anger. We might even have to bite down on our tongues.

But better a bleeding tongue than a family member's wounded heart.

We might have to choose to let go of the need to prove our point, choosing instead to do the right thing: to impart grace and deal with the other person in love and with utmost patience.

We can choose to speak honestly with words that are

direct, but that are also strategically tucked inside an envelope of grace.

When we choose to do this—even though it can be extremely difficult—we model to those closest to us a picture of Christ loving his church. Fights are abandoned. Tempers cool off. Stress simmers down. Our gracious words wash over the other person with love and compassion. We find ourselves faithful to God.

When we lace our speech with grace, healing happens.

So when a family member's behavior threatens to knock the nice right out of us, we can pause before we pounce. (Or better yet, pause, pray, and then don't pounce at all!) Take the advice I sometimes have to give myself: *don't say something permanently painful just because you are temporarily ticked off.*

All the humans you encounter throughout the course of the day are "on purpose" people. God plopped them into your life for a reason. These souls—whether they are of the easy-to-love variety or the scratchy sandpaper kind—can be used by God to mold, reshape, and sometimes stretch our souls as he perpetually crafts us into creations becoming more and more like his Son.

Our people are watching, sizing up how we behave. What will they see? Stirred-up strife—or lovingly covered offenses? Words that incite spats and squabbles? Or speech that soothes and heals?

You choose.

Pssst . . . The correct answer is "g."

Grace.

Today's Takeaways

- *Make it sweet.* How would you rate your speech on the sweetness scale? Does it more closely resemble pure maple syrup or bitter grapefruit juice? If it were a candy, would it be strawberry taffy or a sour, green apple hard candy? Vow today to make your speech sweet like the honeycomb, without a hint of bitter or sour.

- *Help it heal.* Do the words you say and type have restorative qualities? Do they bind wounds and offer a balm of healing? Do you seek to make amends when others have been wronged by what you have said? Make it your goal today to make your interactions with others both health-giving and life-giving.

Lesson for the Lips

How are you doing in the areas of being careful what you drink in and spending time early with the Son? Do you see a correlation between how much time you spend each day drinking in God's Word and how you use your words? Jot a few sentences here that describe your walk with God in this area currently.

_____

_____

_____

_____

Do you have any goals when it comes to spending focused time alone each day with Jesus? What's working? What needs changing? Is it a matter of putting it on your schedule? Of having a friend hold you accountable? Write a few declarative sentences stating what your goals are for spending unrushed time with God each day.

_____

_____

_____

_____

Prayer

Father, thank you for the lessons from the honeycomb. Help me to intentionally carve out time alone each day to meet with you. I want my speech to be sweet and soothing, drawing others to your life-giving gospel. In Jesus's name, amen.

19

FROM FOOTHOLD TO STRONGHOLD

In your anger do not sin: Do not let the sun go
down while you are still angry, and do not give
the devil a foothold. (Eph. 4:26–27)

Our youngest son, Spencer, was a wrestler. Well, only for one season, but it was long enough for me to become a full-fledged wrestling mom. I learned about takedowns, tap outs, and escapes. I sat in the bleachers alongside all the other wrestling parents and yelled phrases like, "Go for the pin!" "Watch for the reversal!" and the ever emphatic, "FINISH HIM!" Not only was the sport entertaining to watch, but it also taught me a lesson about anger and its consequences when it is not dealt with properly. It has to do with our feet.

The feet are important in wrestling. One day I interviewed one of the wrestling coaches at the high school, and I asked him about the mechanics of wrestling. He mentioned that if you can wrap your foot around your opponent's foot, causing him to lose his balance, you can wrestle him to the ground in an all-out pin. In other words, once you get a foothold, you have a chance to get a stronghold, pressing his shoulder blades flat to the mat. And once you exert your strength over your opponent—if you are playing dirty—you can get him in a chokehold, knocking the life and breath right out of him. (Of course, in wrestling this last move is illegal!)

Wow. It's not hard to see the spiritual implications, right?

When Satan gets a foothold, we're in trouble. He wants us to lose our balance. He would love to pin us to the mat, rendering us ineffective for the kingdom. Once we give him a foothold, he can gain a stronghold over us and then go in for the chokehold, finishing us off. Ephesians 4:26–27 tells us how Satan gets that first hold on us: when we fail to deal properly and promptly with our anger.

Using this passage as a template for processing feelings of anger can prevent us from stewing and then striking, which ultimately gives Satan the upper hand. Remember, possessing feelings of anger isn't wrong. What is wrong is when we allow them to fester and then we choose to fight. Weren't we taught long ago as children that fighting is neither healthy nor helpful?

I have found something helpful I can do to stop an argument or prevent one from ever starting in the first place. It not only has to do with my tongue, but with my tone. Often when my tone is combative, I am giving the Devil a foothold. Rather than articulating my anger in an appropriate and straightforward manner, I get caustic, critical—even combative—allowing my volume to escalate and my tone to turn ugly. And then, rather than trying to resolve the issue, I let anger fester and brew, refusing to deal with it and letting time tick off the clock as I get even more ticked off at the person and situation.

Our challenge portion of Scripture today stresses the importance of properly dealing with our feelings of anger. Again—it doesn't say we shouldn't be angry. It doesn't say being mad is a sin. But it does say not taking care of the matter in a godly—and timely—manner is wrong. And when we don't approach the volatile situation correctly, we give Satan a foothold in our lives.

Let's take a lesson from the wrestling world and refuse to give even an inch of ground to the Devil. Rather, let's learn to stop seeing each other as the enemy and realize that the real adversary is Satan. We need to watch for his takedowns, reversals, and pins. With Christ's help we can "FINISH HIM!"

Today's Takeaways

- *It's okay to be angry. It's not okay to let your angry feelings lead to sin.* I'm so thankful Ephesians 4:26–27 makes it clear we are going to feel upset and irritated at times. We must remember that the feelings of fury aren't the issue. The striking out or stewing for days about them are. In between the feelings we experience and the actions of sin is a space—a space where we have a choice: deal with our anger properly or let it lead to sin. Choose your response wisely in the space.

- *Deal with your anger pronto.* While it may help for you to take a timeout and allow your temper to cool off, remember to "not let the sun go down" while you are still hoppin' mad. Simmer down, but be ready to engage in a cool conversation, articulating your feelings without accusations or accosting the other person. Process properly. Seek understanding. Make reconciliation your aim rather than retaliation.

Lesson for the Lips

Think of a time when you did "let the sun go down on your anger." What happened? How long was it until you dealt with your feelings and talked to the person you were upset with? Briefly describe it here:

_____

_____

_____

_____

Now, how could this situation have been handled differently? If you could revisit your actions and take an alternative path, what would you do instead?

Here is a phrase to keep in mind as you interact with others today who may do or say something that causes you to become livid: *attack the problem, not the person.*

Write out this phrase on a sticky note or note card or make it the screen saver on your phone or computer. Memorize it and repeat it back to yourself if you are tempted to lash out.

Prayer

Father, help me to process my angry feelings promptly and in a way that attacks the problem rather than the person. I don't want to give Satan a foothold in my relationships with others. May I learn how to prevent my anger from leading me to sin. In Jesus's name, amen.

20

BUT YOU DON'T KNOW MY FAMILY

If it is possible, as far as it depends on you, live
at peace with everyone. (Rom. 12:18)

Sometimes the digital images I spy during an ordinary day can deflate my spirit and send me into a funk.

A stunning home appears on my television screen, complete with color-coordinated décor, a roaring fire, and furniture that looks as if it was purchased at a high-end department store.

Then I glance around my home.

I see ordinary decorations donning our humble abode, with no quaint wood-burning fireplace (oh, how I wish I had one!). I see no gorgeous couches and chairs, only furniture purchased secondhand from garage sales.

Social media blows up with taunting images too. A lovely tablescape dotted with gourmet foods. A tranquil master bedroom or lovely cottage garden. And on and on. All of these images can make me feel my life and home are "less than" by comparison.

But the images that prompt the most "must be nice" feelings in me are the ones of families gathered together—especially on a holiday. And they're not just gathered. They also appear to be getting along!

Family time around the holidays can be rough. Different personalities, lifestyles, religious beliefs, and political views—even opinions on who should bring the pumpkin pie this year—can all make for an interesting, even explosive, Thanksgiving or yuletide gathering.

I used to enter time with extended family with the goal of everyone behaving—with no outright fights, sarcastic statements, or backhanded comments. While fights didn't always happen, when they did, it was usually due to one particular relative who loves to sling opinions throughout family events. Before each family gathering with this person, I hoped and prayed that no caustic and cruel comments would be directed my way. But rarely did that happen.

Instead I had my mothering skills subtly slammed, my method of mashing potatoes called into question, and worse. As a result, my hopes of a happy family gathering were dashed and my feelings got repeatedly—and deeply—hurt.

Over the years I have found a helpful tool for entering into interactions with the in-laws and the outlaws. I simply apply today's challenge verse from Romans 12:18: "If it is possible, as far as it depends on you, live at peace with everyone."

I am not single-handedly responsible for bringing peace to the family gatherings. I can't close the curtain on every scene of drama. I can't force others to be nice. But I can control *my* words and actions. I can make sure what I say doesn't contribute further to the tension or escalate a minor squabble into a family feud.

As far as it depends on me, I can behave.

I can change the subject. Speak in a calm and collected tone when answering the combative person. Or just simply keep my mouth shut and say nothing at all. I can leave the room and go play with the children. Go into the kitchen and quietly wash the dishes.

I've learned I don't need to say every single thing I'm thinking. Or even half the things I'm thinking!

I can purpose to pray and weigh. Pray that the Lord will help me know if I should speak or remain silent. And weigh each word I do say, asking myself if it is totally appropriate, completely necessary, and ultimately gracious.

Then, when another family gathering is winding down, I can look back and see that I did not contribute to any of the drama that day, but instead I chose—to the best of my ability—to create or keep the peace. I can then put on my coat, give a round of good-bye hugs, and leave the family gathering guilt-free, with no regrets.

Well, except for that second piece of pumpkin pie.

Today's Takeaways

- *Guard your mouth.* Proverbs 13:3 says: "The one who guards his mouth protects his life; the one who opens his lips invites his own ruin" (HCSB). Look at the contrast pointed out in this verse. Guarding your mouth brings protection on your life—from regret, strife, and conflict. Meanwhile, opening your lips indiscriminately invites ruin. When you invite someone to visit, you expect them to come. In the same way we can expect ruin when we have loose lips.

- *Make a concentrated effort.* Romans 14:19 says, "Let us therefore make every effort to do what leads to peace and to mutual edification." Getting along takes effort, especially with the members of our own families. We must not trick ourselves into thinking that relationships come naturally and will always be smooth sailing. Instead, we must expect choppy waters and be prepared to make an effort to get along. You are only responsible for your own behavior. If you make an effort and others do not, it is good to know you have done your part and that God is pleased with your behavior.

Lesson for the Lips

Do you encounter someone at family gatherings whose bad behavior sometimes tempts you to behave poorly in return? Can you think of a specific incident that happened in the past? Briefly describe that time here:

_____

_____

_____

_____

What is your normal tendency when it comes to responding to this person?

How can keeping in mind the instructions in Romans 12:18 help you to alter your behavior around him or her the next time you're together?

Prayer

Father, when interacting with others, especially family members, help me do everything in my ability to live peaceably with everyone. I know it will take effort on my part. Please impart wisdom to me and infuse me with your strength so my actions and reactions are in line with your Word. In Jesus's name, amen.

Bad Speech/ Good Speech

21

THE SNOWBALL OF SENSELESS SPEECH

Avoid godless chatter, because those who indulge in it
will become more and more ungodly. (2 Tim. 2:16)

I remember when my husband and kids attempted to make the biggest snowball ever. The higher than normal winter snowfall accumulation, coupled with three rambunctious children suffering from cabin fever that March, created the perfect setup for such a feat.

With snowsuits zipped tightly, mittens and gloves securely on, and scarves wound tightly around tender little faces, they ventured into our backyard to create the monstrous, icy sphere. The snowball started with just a handful of flakes, packed tightly by my then nine-year-old daughter. One by one she took turns with her six- and three-year-old younger brothers as they rolled the ball all around our backyard, creating a crazy maze of squiggly lines on the winter ground.

The snowball started out sparkly white. But as it grew in size, it needed to be rolled on the ground that began to sport less and less snow. As the snow stuck to the snowball, it exposed what had been hidden underneath it: sticks, dried leaves left over from autumn, an occasional bubblegum wrapper or piece of newspaper. The once pristine snowball even began to pick up tiny stones and bits of dirt as it grew to be ginormous—as our three-year-old described it. When finally it grew too large to be rolled anymore, it was a dingy globe of debris over four feet high! And as you might guess, it took many weeks for the snowball to melt to even half its size. In fact, even after the warm spring weather came, erasing any other trace of snow on the ground or in the trees, the snowball still stood knee-high. It was stubborn and lasting, defiantly refusing to leave.

Today's challenge verse talks about a spiritual snowball we sometimes build in our speech. When we engage in godless chatter, we run the risk of becoming more and more ungodly in our actions. Just what is this type of talk we are to refrain from that is mentioned here on the pages of Scripture?

The New International Version (NIV) translates this phrase "godless chatter." Other translations word it a little differently. The English Standard Version (ESV) reads "irreverent babble." The New American Standard Bible (NASB) calls it "worldly and empty chatter." The New King James Version (NKJV) renders it "profane and idle babblings." The original Greek words mean "an empty discussion of vain and useless matters." As I ponder these renderings, I see a few types of speech that fit this description.

- Gossip. Gossip is any casual or unconstrained conversation that reports about other people. It typically involves details that have not been confirmed as being true. This would certainly fit the description of godless chatter.

- Slander. Slander is another form of harmful rhetoric. It vilifies a person or communicates a false statement that might harm their reputation. By law, if slander is proven, a judgment can be issued against the person speaking such words. Slander is serious business. (Libel is similar, but it is a false and defamatory remark published in written form.)

- Labeling. This form of speech may seem less serious but it is harmful as well and would fall under the category of godless chatter. Labeling is when we slap a title on a person that is not rooted in truth or that is tethered to a harmful stereotype. When we do this we are being prejudiced. Look at the word *prejudice*. Within it we see the phrase "pre-judge." This means we are rendering a judgment before we have all the facts. We are sticking a label on someone just because of their race, religion, gender, country of origin, or other such factor. Labeling is unkind, harmful, and unquestionably falls into the category of godless chatter.

- Petty arguments. Yesterday we talked about quarreling. Petty arguments are useless. We waste our words fighting about trivial matters. Such discussions do not promote Christ nor build up one another. Petty arguments burn up time and are godless. They can also lead to holding grudges and fracturing friendships.

- Idle words. The word *idle* means "without purpose or effect; pointless and without foundation." We can think of idle words like we think of a vehicle stuck in idle— just sitting there, making noise and polluting the air, yet not accomplishing anything or going anywhere. When our words are pointless and without foundation, they are idle words. There is no purpose; we are only filling the air with sound and stink. They are not affecting the situation for good. Idle words also can be godless chatter.

When we engage in any of the above types of speech, we run the risk of our behavior snowballing, becoming even less Christlike "because those who indulge in it will become more and more ungodly" (2 Tim. 2:16). The best way to avoid this snowball effect is to not let any ungodly chatter leave our lips in the first place. May we be prayerful and careful with our speech today, shunning the godless chatter that can lead to a big, ugly mess that takes weeks to melt away.

Today's Takeaways

- *Do not indulge.* To indulge means to allow yourself the pleasure of doing something, usually something you know you should not be doing. When we indulge, at first it's fun. We might even get a little thrill that comes from knowing we shouldn't be doing it. My mother used to say sin is fun for awhile, but then it comes back to bite you. This is very true with godless chatter. It comes back to haunt us, causing problems and damaging relationships. So when you feel that temptation to indulge—even if just a tad—run away fast!

- *Grab yourself a mouth guard.* My son is a football player, and one of his indispensable pieces of equipment is a mouth guard. This shield, when properly worn, makes it nearly impossible for him to talk, but it also prevents injury from occurring if he strikes his mouth on another player or the ground. In the same way, we should ask God to set a guard over our mouths to prevent idle and destructive talk and to guard us from injury (see Psalm 141:3 below).

Lesson for the Lips

Let's try another memory passage today. Write out Psalm 141:3–4, either on paper or electronically, and place it where you will see it often. It may help to set an alarm on your phone to remind you to read and recite the verse, committing it to memory. Then make it your earnest prayer.

> "Set a guard over my mouth, LORD;
>   keep watch over the door of my lips.
> Do not let my heart be drawn to what is evil
>   so that I take part in wicked deeds
> along with those who are evildoers;
>   do not let me eat their delicacies." (Ps.141:3–4)

Prayer

Father, I do not want to indulge in godless chatter, creating a snowball of senseless speech that will be an ugly thing not only in my life, but also in the lives of others. Tap me on the heart. Rearrange my thoughts. Make my speech be sweet to the ears of others, but mostly to yours. In Jesus's name, amen.

22

THE STING OF SEARING SARCASM

How long will you who are simple love your simple
ways? How long will mockers delight in mockery
and fools hate knowledge? (Prov. 1:22)

I hate to admit it, but I have a knack for sarcasm and joking.
As someone who likes to talk and craft clever phrases, as well
as someone who is rather quick on her feet, I can come up
with mocking quips faster than you can open a link to a hilarious comedy video.

Sarcasm and mocking are prevalent in our culture, not
only on television, but also in movies. We spy it online. We
hear it in our high school lunchrooms and around the office
break room. Why, some comedians make a hefty living from
emitting a steady stream of such comedic speech. They're
laughing all the way to the bank.

In the last few years I have become convicted about my

mildly mocking ways. Sure, poking fun might get me a few laughs. Or perhaps get me labeled as witty. But mockery doesn't win me many friends, and it can also fracture family relationships. Besides—most importantly—mockery isn't pleasing to God. So why does sarcasm often rear its jeering head?

First, when we make a sarcastic comment, we can say something without really saying it. It might appear that we are jesting, but in reality we're making a point loud and clear. Through our cynical comment, we may paint another in a bad light: they are habitually late, incessantly sloppy, or not the sharpest crayon in the box. We rattle off a clever phrase that highlights their weakness in neon color, garners a chuckle from those within earshot, and paints us oh-so-witty.

Second, joking and poking fun gets us noticed. In social situations—or even sometimes online—we become the center of attention when we spew sarcasm and make wisecracks. We accomplish our goal of getting all eyes and ears on us—often at the expense of others.

However, more is taking place than the results we see on the surface. Underneath it all, sarcasm stings. And it sears.

Today's challenge verses talk about fools loving mockery and hating knowledge. Mocking isn't tied to the wise but to the fool. Sarcasm might seem harmless because . . . well . . . we are only joking! But it isn't harmless. It's dangerous. Read this: "Like a maniac shooting flaming arrows of death is one who deceives their neighbor and says, 'I was only joking!'" (Prov. 26:18–19).

Wow! What an image! A maniac shooting flaming arrows?

A maniac is out of control, reckless, dangerous, and wild. Flaming arrows are not only sharp, but fiery and hazardous. They can pierce and puncture. They can ignite, causing irreparable damage. This is how Scripture paints a vivid image of our joking, deceptive speech. Yet this type of joking seems like a sport or hobby to the one doing it!

Is all teasing and joking wrong? No. We can make funny comments as long as they don't offend others. However, it is a fine balance to achieve.

And this isn't the only place we are warned about humor gone too far or speech that borders on corrupt. Consider these two verses as well:

"Nor should there be obscenity, foolish talk or coarse joking, which are out of place, but rather thanksgiving" (Eph. 5:4).

And . . .

"Do not let any unwholesome talk come out of your mouths, but only what is helpful for building others up according to their needs, that it may benefit those who listen" (Eph. 4:29).

These verses should help us walk the line when it comes to joking. Not only do they tell us what not to do, but they tell us what our words are to be—edifying and helpful, the kind that build up. Let's aim this week to evaluate our interactions with others—as well as our words *about* others—to make sure we haven't even a hint of improper joking, mocking, or sarcasm.

In other words, let's not be fire-wielding maniacs with bows and arrows.

Today's Takeaways

- *Shoot straight.* In your words, shoot straight. Say what you mean and mean what you say. Pay attention to any tendency you might have to lightheartedly say something that makes a dig, even if in jest. Make it your aim to never utter the phrase "I was only joking" to a person you have offended.

- *Remember your words are like fire and—when shot off recklessly—can ignite a blaze.* Proverbs isn't the only place in the Bible where our words are depicted as fire. James 3 speaks of the tongue being a fire that can corrupt the whole body and set our lives ablaze. It also asserts that a tiny spark of words can become a wildfire. Just envisioning a wildfire and its scorching destruction should cause us to think twice before we let deceptive and sarcastic words escape our lips.

Lesson for the Lips

When it comes to the subjects of sarcasm and coarse jesting, which phrase below best describes you? Circle it.

- I never need to say, "I was only joking."

- I rarely speak in a mocking or sarcastic tone.

- I probably use sarcasm or joking as much as the average person.

- I like to joke around with others, often being sarcastic when I do.

- I am the queen of sarcasm and often use it in my speech.

Can you trace any tense relationships to your sarcastic or inappropriately teasing behavior? How do the verses discussed in today's challenge speak to your behavior in this area? Any changes you desire to make? If so, write them out in a few sentences below.

_____

_____

_____

_____

Now, pick one of the verses for today and write it out in the space provided here. Perhaps seeing it printed in your own handwriting will help you to solidify its importance.

_____

_____

_____

_____

- Proverbs 1:22: "How long will you who are simple love your simple ways? How long will mockers delight in mockery and fools hate knowledge?"

- Proverbs 26:18–19: "Like a maniac shooting flaming

arrows of death is one who deceives their neighbor and says, 'I was only joking!'"

- Ephesians 5:4: "Nor should there be obscenity, foolish talk or coarse joking, which are out of place, but rather thanksgiving."

- Ephesians 4:29: "Do not let any unwholesome talk come out of your mouths, but only what is helpful for building others up according to their needs, that it may benefit those who listen."

Prayer

Father, may I be ever mindful of any of my words that border on sarcasm, coarse jesting, or unwholesome talk. I want my speech to build rather than break, to bless and not badger. Align my words with your will in this area. In Jesus's name, amen.

23

JUST SAY THANKS

Devote yourselves to prayer, being
watchful and thankful. (Col. 4:2)

Wait . . . where is she going?" I asked my then college
boyfriend.

We were strolling with his parents at a festival celebrating Michigan's abundant cherry harvest. His mom—who had been explaining the difference between tart and dark cherries—had stopped talking midsentence and darted off.

I watched her weave through the summertime crowd until she reached her destination. She stopped at the side of a serviceman in uniform and spoke a few words to him. She then gifted him with an impromptu hug and returned to my side, where she finished her discussion of cherries without missing a beat.

For over a quarter century I've watched my (now) mother-in-law thank servicemen and servicewomen wherever she sees them. It can be in the middle of a busy grocery store or in the bleachers of a Friday night football game. She will stop whatever she's doing, walk over to the person, and simply say, "Thank you for serving our country." And then—whether or not they want it—she will present them with one of her grateful hugs.

Often when she turns to walk away, tears fill her eyes. "I tell you," she's declared on more than one occasion, "these young men and women can't ever be thanked enough for all they do for us civilians. We take them for granted every day!"

Her kind gesture touched my heart the very first time I witnessed it. It also inspired me to want to do the same. However, although I am an outgoing and rather chatty gal, I felt a little awkward the first time I decided to give it a try. I wasn't exactly sure what response I would get. Would my words clumsily tumble out of my mouth? Would there be a strange silence? I determined to push past the awkward and try it anyway.

I am thrilled to report that, without fail for over twenty-five years now, I have been greeted with a smile and heartfelt words of appreciation for stopping what I was doing to simply thank a serviceman or servicewoman for sacrificing for our country.

Today's challenge verse tells us the importance of living a prayerful life of observation and thankfulness: "Devote yourselves to prayer, being watchful and thankful" (Col. 4:2).

Learning to take notice of those who serve in our midst and then thanking them can help to grow our prayer life. Often after these encounters, God brings the person back to my mind. I then whisper a prayer for their safety, asking God to make himself very real to them and sustain their loved ones while they are apart during deployment. Because I was watchful and noticed them, and then displayed my thankfulness, I was also granted the honor of praying for these servants.

But it isn't only people in our military who serve. Think through your life on an average day. Who comes across your path? Do you spy the garbage collector faithfully keeping the city clean? The elderly crossing guard safely helping the children scoot across the street to school each morning? The gas station attendant or grocery store clerk doing his or her job with a smile?

Has it ever crossed your mind to simply thank them for what they do so faithfully, without any fanfare? Could you carve out a minute or two in your schedule to add them to your prayers?

Let's use Colossians 4:2 as a template for our ordinary day today. Be prayerful. And watchful. Allow God's Holy Spirit to tap you on the heart and prod you to simply say, "Thank you" to someone who serves. Someone who least expects to be noticed and thanked (or maybe even hugged). Then remember them before your Father as you mention them in prayer.

The small pause in your day and kind gesture of your heart are sure to bring a smile. To their faces . . . and to yours.

Today's Takeaways

- *Thankful words start with words of prayer.* Take note that today's challenge verse begins with being devoted in prayer and then progresses to being thankful. When we spend time in prayer, we are put in our proper place. God is God. We are not. When we recognize we are not in charge of our own lives, and we are not responsible for the many blessings we enjoy each day, it will cause us to be grateful. Our gratefulness for what God has given us will likely spill over into being thankful for others. Then we must open our mouths and let them know we're thankful for them.

- *Pull out your binoculars.* Throughout your day, be watchful. Be a person who notices. Often just pausing for a moment to watch a person's demeanor, or reading between the lines of what's verbally said, will give us a glimpse into the life of someone who could use some kindness or words of thanks. Don't just listen with your ears. Watch with your eyes.

Lesson for the Lips

Think through your ordinary schedule this week. Where will you go? What service providers are you likely to encounter? Jot down one or two of them (even if you don't know their names) here and also on your calendar or in the notes app on your cell phone.

_____

_____

_____

_____

Brainstorm a few simple phrases you could say to each person to show your appreciation for what they do. Then make a point to push past awkward, follow through, and do it!

Write out the following verses in your own handwriting. Then let them serve as a goal for you as you seek to look and listen for ways to thank others.

- "Rejoice always! Pray constantly. Give thanks in everything, for this is God's will for you in Christ Jesus." (1 Thess. 5:16–18 HCSB)

_____

_____

_____

_____

Prayer

Father, may I notice a servant today and stop to genuinely thank him or her. May that person sense your immense love through my simple gesture. In Jesus's name, amen.

24

HELP THEM HIT REFRESH

A generous person will prosper; whoever refreshes
others will be refreshed. (Prov. 11:25)

I was first introduced to Christ when I was a teenager. The
little white steeple on the church at the corner became more
than just a fixture in my Midwestern countryside; it became
a path to a spiritual family. After the pastor's wife invited me
to play on the church's softball team, I soon began hanging
out with an entirely new group of people.

These people loved out loud. They not only welcomed
me with open arms to potlucks and pageants at church, but
they took me into their homes as well. Often I could be found
after school hanging out in one of their kitchens, asking them
questions about my newfound faith. Or a Saturday afternoon
would be spent at their home just blending into their family.
They shared meals with me. And lots of hugs, prayers, and
advice. They shared their very lives.

Once I began to hang around this group of Christians, I had little desire to spend time with most anyone else. My teen years were turbulent—like most teens' are—and I had the added stress of being a child of divorce. My life situation often found me a little down in the dumps. I didn't suffer from all-out depression, but I did have times when I was in definite need of cheering up. And nothing cheered me up faster than to hang out with Mrs. S. or Miss D. for a while. Both of these ladies had a keen knack for helping me find a renewed perspective and face the future with hope in my heart.

I used to think the atmosphere of their homes helped to heal me. Their places were cozy—with a fire in the fireplace warming the room, apple-cinnamon tea steeping in a mug, and a comfy throw waiting for me to snuggle up in while I processed life with them. However, as I look back now, it wasn't so much the ambience and décor of their homes that cheered me as it was the encouraging words they generously spoke to me, refreshing my soul and renovating my perspective on life.

Both of these women stopped whatever they were doing when I came in for a visit. They listened to me talk about the latest drama at school or to my pondering the future and what college I should attend. They not only listened patiently, but responded with words that built me up. Even though I was a baby Christian, they would point out anything good they saw in me, encouraging me in my growth. They would compliment me on my strengths while helping me to work on my weaknesses. And all this was anchored to a firm belief that God had my future already planned out for me and the assurance that he would help that future to unfold if I just continued to trust in him and study his Word.

Going to their homes for these heartfelt pep talks left me refreshed. I'm not sure how I would've made it through those teenage years without them.

Today's challenge verse speaks of such speech. It describes a generous person, one who refreshes others. But what I love most about this verse is the ending; it promises us that when we behave in this way, we will find ourselves refreshed as well. There is just something about encouraging someone else and telling them you believe in them that makes you believe in yourself again too!

Refreshing others isn't confined only to a random verse in Proverbs. We spy it elsewhere in Scripture as well.

In Romans, Paul writes that he longs to visit the church there so "I may come to you with joy, by God's will, and in your company be refreshed" (Rom. 15:32).

In 1 Corinthians, Paul commends three men—whose names I can barely pronounce—for granting him a hearty dose of refreshment: "I was glad when Stephanas, Fortunatus and Achaicus arrived, because they have supplied what was lacking from you. For they refreshed my spirit and yours also. Such men deserve recognition" (1 Cor. 16:17–19).

A man named Onesiphorus was known to often "refresh" others (2 Tim. 1:16).

Philemon was said to bring great joy and encouragement and to refresh "the hearts of the Lord's people" (Philem. 1:7).

If the early church was in need of people who refreshed others with their words, then we certainly are in need of such encouragers today! Will you be one?

Today's Takeaways

- *Help them hit "refresh."* Computers were not around when the New Testament was written. But I can't help getting the image of hitting a Refresh button on the computer when I read the verses that showcase individuals who refreshed the hearts of others, bringing them joy. When we encourage others, we are helping to wipe away the discouraging thoughts and fears that clutter their minds and leave them unable to process or progress. Our words can help them renew their minds and leave the past behind them.

- *Generosity isn't only about money.* When we think of a person who is generous, we might immediately think of monetary gifts. But what if we were generous with our words, freely giving encouragement to those who are discouraged, downtrodden, or just a little glum? Our generous reassurance and support can help build them up so they can once again face life's challenges.

Lesson for the Lips

Has someone in your life used words that refreshed your soul? What did that person say to help you gain new perspective?

Select someone to whom you will speak words of encouragement today, helping to refresh them and renew their hope for the future. Write that person's name here:

_____

Now jot down how you will do this. Will you make a phone call? Send a handwritten note in the mail? Speak it in person? Be sure to follow through on your intentions. Not only will you brighten that someone's day, but your heart will be refreshed as well.

_____
_____
_____
_____

Prayer

Father, I want to be known as someone who is generous with words of encouragement, refreshing the hearts of others. May I be on the lookout for the weary, the worried, and others who need such a boost today. Most importantly, may the words I speak glorify you as they encourage them. In Jesus's name, amen.

25

TO TELL THE TRUTH

Each of you must put off falsehood and speak truthfully to
your neighbor, for we are all members of one body. (Eph. 4:25)

When I was a little girl, my family sometimes watched a
popular game show called *To Tell the Truth*. The show featured a panel of four celebrities whose job was to identify a
contestant who served in an unusual role or who had a unique
occupation or rare experience. The contestant sat alongside
two other people who acted as impostors, pretending to be
the special guest. The famous panelists would question the
three contestants, trying to discover who the impostors were
and who the real guest was. The fakes were allowed to lie, but
the central character was sworn "to tell the truth." After ques-
tioning, the panel attempted to identify which of the three
challengers was indeed telling the truth. Often one of the
impostors was so convincing it threw the celebrities off and
they chose the wrong person.

It seems that today our culture is engaged in a monumental game of *To Tell the Truth*. Not so long ago cultural standards and expected behaviors were mostly in line with Scripture, but today that's just not the case. Our culture often asserts wrongheaded beliefs, calling good evil and evil good. What should be our response as followers of Christ to the often misguided standards of our day? We need to expose those standards as lies by pointing to the eternal truths given to us in Scripture. Let me give you a few examples.

- Our culture asserts that the more material things you have, the happier and more fulfilled you will be. After all, as a popular bumper sticker claims, "The one who dies with the most toys wins!" However, God's Word says we are not to love the things of this world (1 John 2:15–17), but to store up for ourselves treasures in heaven (Matt. 6:20).

- Our culture celebrates being drunk, joking about it and making light of it. Scripture, however, teaches us not to be drunk with alcohol but instead to be filled with the Spirit (Eph. 5:18).

- Society not only pokes fun at fidelity, but encourages adultery. Websites devoted to arranging affairs for married people even exist. However, God's Word says we are to have one spouse and, barring any biblical grounds for divorce, to stick with that one spouse (Matt. 19:4–9). Again, eternal truth.

As believers in Jesus and bearers of the gospel, the words we speak should accurately reflect the truth of Scripture. But sometimes it's hard to speak up for the truth in the midst of a culture steeped in lies. We find ourselves alone. We may get labeled as an oddball. We can even lose friends or distance our coworkers because they believe our thinking is out of date and our beliefs are sorely out of touch.

However, we are called to believe, live, and speak the truth. Consider these verses:

- Psalm 15:1–2: "LORD, who may dwell in your sacred tent? Who may live on your holy mountain? The one whose walk is blameless, who does what is righteous, who speaks the truth from their heart."

- Romans 1:25: "They exchanged the truth about God for a lie, and worshiped and served created things rather than the Creator—who is forever praised. Amen."

- Zechariah 8:16: "These are the things you are to do: Speak the truth to each other; and render true and sound judgment in your courts."

- Jeremiah 7:28: "Therefore say to them, 'This is the nation that has not obeyed the LORD its God or responded to correction. Truth has perished; it has vanished from their lips.'"

- Proverbs 8:6–8: "Listen, for I have trustworthy things to say; I open my lips to speak what is right.

My mouth speaks what is true, for my lips detest wickedness. All the words of my mouth are just; none of them is crooked or perverse."

Others are watching our behavior and listening to our speech. If we are to accurately reflect Scripture, we will often find ourselves at odds with the world's thinking and in direct opposition to what it says is acceptable, right, and true. Will those in our lives be able to tell the impostor from the real deal? Will they be pointed to the One who is the way, the truth, and the life?

This is no game; our words are on trial. Will they tell the truth? I am reminded of a little poem by Paul Gilbert that I learned shortly after I became a believer:

> *You are writing a gospel a chapter each day,*
> *By the things that you do and the words that you say.*
> *Others will read what you write, whether faulty or true.*
> *Say, what is the gospel according to you?*

Today's Takeaways

- *To speak the truth, we need to study and know the truth.* Never at any time in history have Christians had so much biblical content at their disposal. We have Christian books, Bible studies, and blogs written by believers. We spy serene-looking photographs with spiritual sayings on social media. But often we neglect going to the source of all truth itself—the Bible. Let's be intentional to find out what the Bible has to say about certain issues, not just popular blogger so-and-so or our favorite famous Bible teacher.

- *Be a truth teller, but don't forget to be kind.* While some of us may need a nudge to step up and tell the truth boldly, others of us sometimes bark out the truth in an unloving manner and need to learn to take a step back and wrap truth in a cushion of kindness. Yes, Scripture calls us to be truth tellers, but it also calls us to be gentle and respectful.

Lesson for the Lips

In what areas does the world have totally opposite standards from what is put forth in Scripture to be right and true? List a few below.

_____

_____

_____

_____

Using an online search or site such as BibleGateway, locate verses that show God's viewpoint on those issues. Write out the references below.

_____

_____

_____

_____

What are some guidelines to keep in mind when discussing what is true with those who believe differently from what the Bible teaches? Keep these guidelines in mind as you interact with such people in the future.

Prayer

Father God, your Word is truth. You are truth. Jesus is the way, the truth, and the life, and no one comes to you but through him. May my life boldly reflect this to others while also delivering the message with grace and kindness. In Jesus's name, amen.

When to Be Silent and When to Speak Up

26

WHEN YOU *THINK* YOU KNOW WHY: IT'S TIME TO BE SILENT

Fools base their thoughts on foolish assumptions, so
their conclusions will be wicked madness; they chatter
on and on. No one really knows what is going to happen;
no one can predict the future. (Eccl. 10:13–14 NLT)

Have you ever experienced a tragedy, only to have someone
try to explain *why* it happened to you—even though they
didn't know what they were talking about? It's frustrating, to
say the least. Depending on their diagnosis of your problems,
the friendship could be forever fractured, all because they
couldn't contain their assumptions.

The Bible has an example of this scenario. Remember
when Job lost everything? He had friends willing to
explain his situation to him. Now, Job's friends made some

exceptional moves. They came to see Job. They intended to show him sympathy and comfort. They even tore their robes and sat silently with him for a week. I don't know about you, but though I might have sent a sympathy card or taken over a tasty casserole, I have neither torn my clothes nor been silent for a week! This is quite an expression of concern. However, what they did next discredits their status as BFFs. Job's friends went on to explain everything to Job as if he wasn't familiar with God's ways. A brief portion of this is seen here, when Job's friend Zophar is speaking.

> "Should I remain silent while you babble on? When you mock God, shouldn't someone make you ashamed? You claim, 'My beliefs are pure,' and 'I am clean in the sight of God.' If only God would speak; if only he would tell you what he thinks!" (Job 11:3–5 NLT)

I see five reasons why Job's friends should have been silent in this situation—and why in the face of suffering we need to choose silence too.

1. Friends need support, not lecture. Remember how, when you were a child, your mom told you not to jump off the swings? But you did it anyway, got hurt, and went crying back to her? Your mom did one of two things: she either hugged you silently or said, "I told you so." Which was more comforting? If I were Job, I wouldn't want anyone to say anything except for a simple prayer.

2. Every story has a supernatural side. You've heard the phrase "There's always two sides to a story." No one, not

even Job, knew what had transpired between God and the Devil before Job experienced this intense trial. In Job 1, God bragged to the Devil about Job, calling him a blameless and upright man. The Devil scoffed, claiming Job loved God only because God had blessed him, and that Job would curse God if he lost everything.

None of Job's friends knew about this conversation. How then could they thoroughly and accurately describe Job's situation? They couldn't.

You don't know the supernatural side of any story. I don't either. So when we are tempted to speak about why something happened, we must consider that we do not know the supernatural side of the story. As Ecclesiastes 10:13 says, "Fools base their thoughts on foolish assumptions" (NLT).

3. We might be remembered only for our response. We never know when something we say or do will become the very thing others use to define us. It's a harsh statement, but please seriously consider this: we don't know Job's friends for their generosity or their accomplishments; we know them only for what they said. Our words are more eternally indelible than what we realize when we say them. For this reason, we must consider what it would be like if our words were written down for others to learn from for countless years ahead.

Would your words be humble and few, or would they be an example of what *not* to do? Can't decide? Surrender yourself to silence.

4. Our words could incite God's anger. We don't like to talk about God's anger, but that doesn't make it any less real. Job 42:7 records, "After the LORD had finished speaking

to Job, he said to Eliphaz the Temanite: 'I am angry with you and your two friends, for you have not spoken accurately about me, as my servant Job has'" (NLT). God's disapproval of Job's friends ignites a sense of caution within me. Does it do the same for you? It's difficult to always speak accurately about the Lord, because even if we've read the Bible, God still possesses knowledge beyond our understanding. So again, staying silent is the best option.

5. When we practice purposeful silence, we create space for the suffering person to reflect, process, and grieve. It also allows them to be the one to talk—when they are ready. It makes room for them rather than imposing ourselves on them or placing the focus wrongly on us and our advice.

Pondering these points, it's clear how valuable supportive and reverent silence is in a situation where someone is suffering. Take heart, though. Not every situation calls for silence. We'll talk more about that in the coming days.

Today's Takeaways

- *Consider the supernatural.* Ask yourself, "Could there be more to this story?" Remember that you are not all-knowing. Pray to the only One who can see a situation from all angles. Ask him if there is anything beneficial to say to the one hurting. When in doubt, trust that supportive silence is best.

- *How do you want others to remember you?* When it comes to the words you say to others during a tragedy or tough time, how do you want to be remembered? As one who encouraged and spoke God's truths that brought hope? You probably don't want to be known as someone who brought confusion and discouragement to the situation.

Lesson for the Lips

Reflect on a time you said something without knowing all the details. Or reflect upon a time someone tried explaining your situation to you when they didn't know the full story. How did it feel? What was your response? Take some time to remember. Decide to choose silence if there is any chance of hurting someone else.

Prayer

Dear heavenly Father, you have the perfect view of everything. Only you know the explanation for why things happen. Help me not to respond in a way I will regret. Help me resist the urge to explain to others when I could simply sit quietly and comfort my friends by listening. I don't always have the self-control to remember to be still, but with your help I can calmly and silently walk with my friends through their trials. In Jesus's name, amen.

27

WHEN YOU KNOW BETTER: IT'S TIME TO BE SILENT

They kept quiet because on the way they had argued
about who was the greatest. (Mark 9:34)

Remember saying something somewhat naughty when you
thought your parents weren't within earshot? Remember the
feeling when you realized your mom or dad had heard you?
Somehow parents can hear unsavory comments through
closed doors or piles of luggage in a cramped van. Anybody?
Parents sense when their kids are doing or saying something
wrong. Similarly, but of course on a supernatural level, Jesus
can hear everything we say, even though we can't see him.

Do you think the disciples knew Jesus was overhearing their
conversation when they began to discuss who was the greatest
among them? I think they forgot. We all forget Jesus is right
here, don't we? So sometimes it helps when he turns to us and
says, "What was that you were saying?" In Mark 9 we have this:

They left that place and passed through Galilee. Jesus did not want anyone to know where they were, because he was teaching his disciples. He said to them, "The Son of Man is going to be delivered into the hands of men. They will kill him, and after three days he will rise." But they did not understand what he meant and were afraid to ask him about it. They came to Capernaum. When he was in the house, he asked them, "What were you arguing about on the road?" But they kept quiet because on the way they had argued about who was the greatest. Sitting down, Jesus called the Twelve and said, "Anyone who wants to be first must be the very last, and the servant of all." (vv. 30–35)

Look at this! Jesus just prophesied his own death and resurrection, but instead of responding to this profound revelation, the disciples let it pass without comment or question. But then when with something they really didn't need to figure out (say, who was the greatest among them), they argued about it. In other words, Jesus just said, "I'm going to die!" and their response was "Uh, that's weird. Now, will you tell me how important I am, because so-and-so disagrees with me!"

I sound critical, but if I'm honest, I have to admit I do the same thing. It goes something like this . . .

I will dutifully read a portion of God's Word, but instead of taking the time to pray about it or joyfully receiving the truth of the gospel, I just let it pass. I let the Word walk on by. In a few hours, however, I find myself caught up in an argument with my kids, interrogating them about who took the car for how long and why there wasn't any gas left in the tank. In that situation, did I let the good news of God's Word penetrate my spirit, my thoughts, and my subsequent actions? No.

I'm afraid so often we are like the disciples. Jesus tells us something earth-shattering about himself and then we get wrapped up in ourselves instead of soaking up what he just said! When Jesus speaks to us, it's always for good reason. We shouldn't hear the words and then fail to pursue them.

Apparently the disciples couldn't agree on who was the greatest, but they did know better than to argue with Jesus. How do I know? Because when Jesus asked them what they were talking about, they were silent. It goes back to when our parents asked us, "What are you doing?" As children, sometimes we didn't have the heart to answer, because we knew what we were doing was wrong. Sometimes we have to think ahead and ask ourselves, "If Jesus were to confront me about this conversation, would I feel regretful?"

The wonderful thing Jesus did was teach them. He didn't point a finger at them or speak in a condescending tone. He saw their hearts and gave them an illustration, patiently answering their question by telling them that the greatest person must be the servant of all.

The Bible says, "Do nothing out of selfish ambition or vain conceit. Rather, in humility value others above yourselves, not looking to your own interests but each of you to the interests of the others" (Phil. 2:3–4). When you find yourself in a fruitless argument or when you say something stupid and self-serving even when you know better, turn your focus back to the Suffering Servant. Only he can change your heart and renew your perspective.

Today's Takeaways

- *Choose better.* If you happen to find yourself in a conversation heading toward an argument or a selfish pursuit, listen to the voice of Jesus asking, "Now, what was that you were saying?" Often this reminder will help us to silence statements better left unsaid. If we know better than to say something, we must choose better.

- *Talk to Jesus instead of arguing with others.* When we are in the midst of a tense or even heated conversation, let's fight the urge to argue. Instead, let's talk to Jesus, asking him to guide our words—or help us keep silent.

Lesson for the Lips

Whenever you're in a conversation and someone says, "Excuse me?" or "Can you repeat that?" it might be the Holy Spirit giving you a chance to think about whether you should repeat what you just said. We can also use this approach with others. If someone else says something offensive, give them another chance by asking them to repeat themselves. In so doing they might hear the Holy Spirit's voice urging them to refrain or reword. If you have a chance to try this today, do so and record the results here:

_____

_____

_____

_____

Prayer

Dear heavenly Father, you are such a kind and gracious Father to allow us second chances, even in our speech. Don't let me miss the second chances you might give me in a situation when someone else says, "What is that you were saying?" Thank you for this simple phrase to remind me that I can rethink my words and, finding them wrong, transform them into words pleasing to you. In Jesus's name, amen.

28

WHEN YOU CAN HELP (AND THERE'S NOTHING IN IT FOR YOU): IT'S TIME TO SPEAK UP

Speak up for those who cannot speak for themselves,
for the rights of all who are destitute. (Prov. 31:8)

There is more than one kind of destitute. You can be lacking financial means, but you can also be spiritually destitute. Those who are spiritually destitute lack spiritual answers. They might be intellectual or wealthy, but they are poor in the riches of Jesus Christ.

Naaman was a man I believe was spiritually destitute. That is, before one little girl changed his story.

We meet Naaman in 2 Kings 5.

Now Naaman was commander of the army of the king of Aram. He was a great man in the sight of his master and highly regarded, because through him the LORD had given victory to Aram. He was a valiant soldier, but he had leprosy. Now bands of raiders from Aram had gone out and had taken captive a young girl from Israel, and she served Naaman's wife. She said to her mistress, "If only my master would see the prophet who is in Samaria! He would cure him of his leprosy." (vv.1–3)

We can pull so many interesting aspects out of this short account. Anytime I re-examine a passage in the Bible, different words or phrases stand out. This time I see the phrase "if only."

This girl was a captive. She was taken from her home. She had lost everything and was now in a foreign place away from her community of faith and apart from whatever comforts she once knew. If anyone were to peek into her situation, they would say "if only" in regard to her! They would say, "If only she would be set free," or "If only she could be reunited with her parents," or "If only she didn't have to serve in this household." But no. No one looked at this girl and said that. *Instead, the girl looked at Naaman and said "if only."*

She had something he didn't. She knew where to go for healing. I love, also, that she had no doubt about it. She didn't say, "I'd suggest Naaman pay a visit to the prophet," or even "Hey, give this a shot; it couldn't hurt." No. She says, "He would cure him of his leprosy." Here you have a child teaching a commander of an army. Isn't this beautiful?

As if that's not quite enough, there's a precise lesson in this story for our words: speak up for those who cannot speak for themselves.

Naaman didn't have a speech problem, but he couldn't speak up for the true needs of his heart. You must speak up for those who are spiritually destitute and don't know where to find true healing. If you don't, who will? Perhaps you were placed directly in your situation to speak up for a desperate soul.

We don't know if this girl was rewarded. The Bible doesn't say anything about Naaman bringing back gifts for her or thanking her. As far as I can see, there was nothing in it for this girl. She spoke up because she wanted Naaman to be well.

What happened to Naaman in this story? He listened. He went to the prophet and ultimately found the healing he longed for. His journey started somewhere so small and so unselfish. Instead of pleading for her release, this girl declared the path of healing for Naaman. She lived out Philippians 2:3–4, which says, "Do nothing out of selfish ambition or vain conceit. Rather, in humility value others above yourselves, not looking to your own interests but each of you to the interests of the others."

We cannot allow the volume of captivity to drown out the subtle cries of the spiritually needy. Somehow, we must rest in knowing that Jesus is with us and wants to reach those around us. We may not be compensated, set free, or even given the mention of our full name. But God remembers our story. God remembered this girl's story. She spoke up for someone else's need even though, to our knowledge, no one spoke up for her situation.

How humbling to consider that saying something out of compassion can set another person free from a lifelong prison. "If only" we would compassionately speak up for the spiritual needs of others and care less about our own physical discomforts.

Today's Takeaways

- *In the midst of captivity, stay focused.* As followers of Christ, we are never left as orphans. We are more than conquerors in Christ Jesus our Lord (Rom. 8:37). However, in this world we will have trouble (John 16:33). We will experience persecution and physical hardship. When you find yourself in a physically or emotionally challenging environment, don't forget your spiritual freedom. You are rich. Rich enough that you can still look around and give life to those God has intentionally placed on your path.

Lesson for the Lips

When was the last time you felt the urge to speak up for the spiritually destitute, but didn't because of fear? Write down your memory.

_____

_____

_____

_____

Ask the Holy Spirit to remind you of a promise from his Word to squelch this fear. If nothing comes to mind, do a simple Google search for "verses about courage from the Bible." You'll find some helpful links with some powerful Scriptures. Choose one and jot it down here:

_____

_____

_____

_____

Prayer

Dear heavenly Father, so many times I am tempted to focus on myself, especially when I'm uncomfortable. Please allow me to look around and speak up for those who are spiritually destitute. Allow me to have eyes on others' hearts and not just on my own situation. Thank you for this lesson. In Jesus's name, amen.

29

WHEN ONLY GOD KNOWS WHAT JUST HAPPENED: IT'S TIME TO BE SILENT

Then a cloud appeared and covered them, and
a voice came from the cloud: "This is my Son,
whom I love. Listen to him!" (Mark 9:7)

When was the last time you were rendered speechless? Can you remember? It's been a long time for me. Not because I'm a calloused person, but because we live in a crazy world. Amazing or horrific events don't carry the same impact they would have twenty years ago because of one, culture-shifting juggernaut: social media.

Because of social media, we see everything almost immediately. Hilarious viral videos, tragic rollover accidents, or even surprisingly candid moments—it's all right there for the world to view and process. Still, even with the broad range of outrageous visuals we have access to, I have never seen a viral video without a comment. Despite any sense of shock, we usually come up with a response. But is a response always necessary? What if we surrendered ourselves to silence, wonder, and awe more often?

Jesus's disciple Peter had access to all the footage needed for a viral video, but thankfully, no one would have to huddle around a small screen or create a hashtag for an event too holy for such a thing. We have the most reliable source, God's Word, to explain to us exactly what happened at Jesus's transfiguration.

> After six days Jesus took Peter, James and John with him and led them up a high mountain, where they were all alone. There he was transfigured before them. His clothes became dazzling white, whiter than anyone in the world could bleach them. And there appeared before them Elijah and Moses, who were talking with Jesus. Peter said to Jesus, "Rabbi, it is good for us to be here. Let us put up three shelters—one for you, one for Moses and one for Elijah." (He did not know what to say, they were so frightened.) Then a cloud appeared and covered them, and a voice came from the cloud: "This is my Son, whom I love. Listen to him!" Suddenly, when they looked around, they no longer saw anyone with them except Jesus. As they were coming down the mountain, Jesus gave them orders not to tell anyone

what they had seen until the Son of Man had risen from the dead. (Mark 9:2–9)

Truthfully, I probably would have done the same thing Peter did. I don't like the fact that I always react verbally, but my words curiously find every event a worthy occasion to attend. In this passage we see that Peter's blurted-out words were birthed from fear. "He [Peter] did not know what to say, they were so frightened" (v. 6). I find it interesting that Peter became the spokesperson for everyone's fear. Did the others want to put a voice to their fear, or did they reserve the right to quietly process this sight? We don't know, because Peter seized the opportunity to speak.

When Peter suggested putting up shelters, Jesus didn't respond. Although Jesus would've known what to say, he remained silent and allowed his Father to speak on his behalf. A cloud covered them, and God said, "This is my Son, whom I love. Listen to him!" (v. 7).

What is the very next thing Jesus says? He tells them not to say anything until he has risen from the dead. So this is another lesson about not speaking. Let's step back from the passage and revisit the original thought for today. Why don't we allow some moments to render us speechless?

I believe we have to *learn* to shut our mouth and allow the awe of God to fill our heart and mind. Silence is a practice. We discipline ourselves toward the stillness. But God knows we need this discipline because he commands it: "Be still, and know that I am God" (Ps. 46:10).

In the book of Revelation, we have a stunning example

of silence as a response. "When he opened the seventh seal, there was silence in heaven for about half an hour" (Rev. 8:1).

Magnificent things happen, and they don't always need our commentary.

If there is a time to *be still and know,* how often do you find yourself keeping that appointment?

Today's Takeaways

- *Practice silence.* Not every viral video should be shared or commented on. Not every Bible study requires a lecture. Not every sermon requires a verbal response. Divine revelation meets listeners before it meets talkers, so try today to cultivate the practice of silence.

Lesson for the Lips

Whenever I'm in a Bible study group, I love contributing. However, one time God told me to take a backseat. He told me to be a listener for the entire nine-week Bible study. It was hard. I wanted to jump in on almost every question. But I paused and watched as plenty of other people from the group added valuable content to the conversation. What if you decided to attend the next Bible study as a listener? I think you would be surprised by what you learned.

Prayer

Father, I love to comment. But I am asking you to please give me the self-control to practice stillness and silence. When something happens that should elicit awe, I pray I will soak up the moment instead of spewing words spontaneously. There is a time to be silent, and I pray I'll find myself more and more comfortable with a silent and reverent response. In Jesus's name, amen.

30

WHEN YOU KNOW THEY NEED TO KNOW: IT'S TIME TO SPEAK UP

"Go and make disciples of all nations, baptizing
them in the name of the Father and of the Son
and of the Holy Spirit." (Matt. 28:19)

My heart was beating wildly, the sweat was pumping furiously, and my words were coming out shaky at best. I was about to speak with the president of my college about a serious situation I observed concerning a faculty member. I knew the truth, but I was apprehensive in speaking up because I feared the administrator might not believe me or might automatically side with the professor. This experience reinforced for me this truth: whenever God has called me to say something unpopular in any setting, it is a scary experience.

No matter how young or old you are, most likely you can

recall a time when the Lord called you to stand up for your faith by confronting the faithless. Elijah did this, leaving an extraordinary example for us.

Elijah did many miraculous things in his time. Our story today is the account of his facing the Baal prophets on Mount Carmel. This story is so rich! Read the full account in 1 Kings 18; then look at this verse:

> Elijah went before the people and said, "How long will you waver between two opinions? If the LORD is God, follow him; but if Baal is God, follow him." But the people said nothing. (1 Kings 18:21)

Elijah was outnumbered 450 to 1. I find it challenging to stand up to one person of another faith let alone 450! Why would he do this? How would he do this? I believe Elijah *had* to do this because he knew *they needed to know* what's what.

Within our circles of friends, there is a time to let them share about their faith and their beliefs, including friends of other faiths. Don't get me wrong. There is always time for listening. But when God tells you it's time for them to know who he is, then it's time to speak up. This could happen in a number of ways, but in that moment, you cannot shrink back. As Hebrews 10:39 says, "We do not belong to those who shrink back and are destroyed, but to those who have faith and are saved." Sister, let's be encouraged by Elijah's example.

Elijah could have stopped after suggesting they follow the one true God. He could have just left that idea hanging in the air. But he didn't. Elijah went on to challenge the Baal prophets. They would have to prepare a sacrifice; then

Elijah would prepare a sacrifice. Each side would call upon their god, and the god who answered by fire would be the one true God.

Here is the first observation. Someone can only say they believe in God, but then someone can say *and* act in accordance with their belief. Elijah said it, but then he really put his faith out there on the line.

In this story, fire comes down from heaven and God shows himself powerfully! Elijah speaks up and God shows up. This is how the story concludes: "When all the people saw this, they fell prostrate and cried, 'The LORD—he is God! The LORD—he is God!'" (1 Kings 18:39).

How do we apply this to our lives? Realize the need for God. Share testimonies. Share Bible verses. But we will still need to put ourselves out there for God, and we will always need him!

So how do you know when it's a time to step out with your faith or when it's a time to listen?

You will feel it.

Deep inside, *you will know they need to know.*

I think we sometimes forget the Great Commission: "Go and make disciples of all nations, baptizing them in the name of the Father and of the Son and of the Holy Spirit" (Matt. 28:19). We are called to make others into disciples. So when we sit with our friends or talk to our neighbors, we must not lose sight of showing them God. It will involve speaking up. It will involve putting our faith out there and being brave. In our words and in our actions, may they see God for exactly who he is.

Today's Takeaways

- *Don't shrink back.* When you feel nervous about telling your friends about God, remember Hebrews 10:39: "We do not belong to those who shrink back." We serve a mighty God. We serve a God who keeps his promises. We serve a God who cares about his glory. Let me encourage you to not shrink back when you hear that voice urging you to share what you know is true!

- *Have courage when you're outnumbered.* Elijah was one man facing 450 prophets of Baal. More than likely, you won't be in a situation where you are facing this kind of hostile crowd. But if you find yourself there, know that someone else has been there who proved himself faithful in these circumstances. You can too.

Lesson for the Lips

We can do only so much sitting back and silent witnessing. Think of just one person in your life who does not know the Lord. Pray. Bring his or her name before our Father. Today might not be the right time to share with them, but ask God to bring about an opportunity soon.

Prayer

Dear heavenly Father, give me courage to speak up at just the right time. Allow me the faith to put myself out there. Please soften the heart of the person I was just thinking of to accept the words you give me. Keep Elijah's story of fiery faith at the center of my heart. In Jesus's name, amen.

Making Our Words Both Sweet and Salty

31

DO OR DIE: THE SWEET
WORDS OF ABIGAIL

"See, I have obeyed your voice, and I have
granted your petition." (1 Sam. 25:35 ESV)

Have you ever been in a do-or-die situation? A situation
where the outcome could be tragic if words were not deli-
cately communicated? Maybe your job was in danger of
being eliminated if you didn't find a way to explain its importance to the mission of your company. Or maybe a precious
relationship would implode if you didn't find the right words
to defuse the situation. In certain extreme cases, the "do or
die" can be literal—people's lives could be on the line if you
don't respond wisely.

That was the situation for Abigail. Do you remember
her? She was the "beautiful and intelligent" woman who first
appeared in 1 Samuel 25:3. Her husband, Nabal, was rich,
but he wasn't the kindest person on the desert block. The

Bible says he was "surly and mean" (v. 3). David sent men to request food from Nabal in return for watching his flocks. Nabal denied his request, and he didn't win a "Gracious and Suave Response of the Year" award either.

Nabal said, "Who is David? Who is the son of Jesse? There are many servants these days who are breaking away from their masters. Shall I take my bread and my water and my meat that I have killed for my shearers and give it to men who come from I do not know where?" (vv. 10–11 ESV). So David's young men turned away, went back, and told him all this. David's response? He told his guys, "Each of you strap on his sword!" (v. 13).

Did you catch how many times Nabal said "my" or "I" in that short response? "My bread" . . . "my water" . . . "my meat" . . . "I killed" . . . "my shearers . . ." I find this interesting, but I also find David's reactionary words telling. He was quick to get angry and immediately instructed his men to wield their weapons. (Sometimes we, too, are swift to wield the slicing sword of our tongue in a disagreement, aren't we?)

Nabal's selfish and proud words elicited violent words and fatal intentions from David.

Abigail caught wind of what was about to happen and suddenly found herself in a true "do-or-die" scenario. And here it is: Abigail's words changed David's mind.

Seriously.

She rushed out to David with two things: generous gifts and sweet words. She took two hundred loaves of bread, two skins of wine, five butchered sheep, and a generous portion of other goodies. She approached humbly, first bowing and asking for permission to speak. She took the blame on herself and for Nabal. She didn't go as a narcissist, yakking all about herself and her belongings as Nabal did, but instead spoke highly of David.

David then praised God. He calmly said to Abigail, "Go up in peace to your house. See, I have obeyed your voice, and I have granted your petition" (v. 35 ESV). How did she manage to convince David to refrain from killing all the men folk in her family? I believe she did this through properly seasoning her speech as suitable for the occasion.

Now, we might not meet a man who's bringing four hundred armed men to wipe away our family name, but we might experience moments when a job, a relationship, or even a life is on the line. I wonder, in those moments, will we attack, using belligerent anger to try to get our way? Or will we get defensive, implying we are the victim and the other is at fault? Or maybe we'll just freak out and surrender ourselves to disaster!

Friends, in those times remember Abigail, whose sweet words and divine wisdom saved her.

Today's Takeaways

- *Humility is always the best start.* Nabal started with a proud response. Abigail started with humility. Abigail survived to the end of the chapter, which is longer than Nabal did . . . just sayin'.

- *Don't be too quick to draw your sword.* Unlike David, Abigail didn't gather anyone to fight. Her quick response was verbal and tangible giving. She was wealthy. She probably had the resources to attack or to defend herself, but she didn't act or talk in a combative or defensive way. She was sweet, which is exactly what this occasion called for.

- *Actions pair well with words.* Just as cheese pairs well with fruit or pumpkin pie pairs well with a cloud of real whipped cream, generous words pair well with generous actions. Both are sensational to the recipient and are more likely to yield a positive outcome! If you face a threatening person or situation, remember that God has already provided you with everything you need. Go to that person or situation knowing you are equipped with God's strength, wisdom, and peace.

Lesson for the Lips

Consider this: the Bible says Abigail "made haste" to take her gift and go speak to David (1 Sam. 25:18 ESV). Do you think this was Abigail's first time speaking sweetly in a precarious situation? We all need to practice speaking sweetly in the *little* trials so if a true do-or-die situation ever arises we will know what to say, how to say it, and whether to say nothing at all. Can you think of a small situation where you are currently being called to speak sweetly? Briefly describe it here:

_____

_____

_____

_____

By cultivating the habit of sweet speech in lesser situations, we will be better prepared to speak wisely in greater ones.

Prayer

Dear Lord, let me remember Proverbs 15:1, which says, "A gentle answer turns away wrath, but a harsh word stirs up anger." In the challenges I encounter this week, let me meet them with gifts and good words. Whether I am speaking sweetly to myself or to an enemy, let me always speak the truth in love. I pray that by my giving sweet and generous responses, the outcomes of this week's trials will be positive and peaceful. In Jesus's sweet name, amen.

32

POURING SALT ON A WOUND: THE SALTY WORDS OF DAVID

David said to Nathan, "I have sinned
against the LORD." (2 Sam. 12:13)

We've discussed the uses of salt in a previous chapter. However, there is one use I didn't mention. Are you familiar with the phrase "pouring salt on a wound"? It means you are taking a bad situation and making it worse. Or you have hurt someone's feelings badly and are only causing them further pain. This phrase has negative connotations, but salt on a wound is not all bad.

A *little* salt on a fresh cut can keep bacteria from growing and start the healing process. Likewise, a bit of salty speech might be the best thing to cleanse a swollen and "sin-fected" heart.

So who in the Bible had an infection? Well, the flawed hero David immediately comes to mind.

POURING SALT ON A WOUND: THE SALTY WORDS OF DAVID

One evening King David was looking out over his king-dom and saw a lady out bathing in only her birthday suit. David wanted this woman. *Really* wanted her. Although David was already married, it didn't stop him from sending for her. Some greater-than-PG-rated things happened that evening, and Bathsheba (the babe from the bathtub) became pregnant. And here's where the injury really gets severe . . . *she's already married too.* And who is she married to but a man fighting a war FOR KING DAVID! (Mercy, is it getting hot in here?)

So David has done a bad thing. David has done a very, very bad thing. But it gets worse when he learns Bathsheba is pregnant and tries to cover up his sin. David requests that Bathsheba's husband, Uriah, be brought to him. He tells Uriah to go home, take a break from battle, and spend an evening with the missus. He hopes Uriah will sleep with Bathsheba so David's baby will be mistaken for Uriah's child.

David thinks this ruse might be his one-way ticket out of consequence town until he realizes Uriah never went home that night. David then unsuccessfully tries again to get Uriah to go home and cozy up to his woman. When this fails, David sends Uriah to the front lines of battle to be killed, and killed he is. David's heart is infected with lust, dishonesty, pride, adultery, and finally murder; his wound has turned gangrenous.

Then a man named Nathan goes to David and clev-erly tells him a story that opens David's eyes to what he has done. Using salty speech, Nathan confronts David with his sin, and instead of responding with more lies and more evil, David is struck to the heart and in return speaks these salty words of confession: "I have sinned against the LORD" (2 Sam. 12:13).

Why are words of confrontation and confession salty? Because they are words of truth, and truthful words sometimes sting but always help heal.

David suffered the consequences of his actions, which you can read more about in 2 Samuel 12:14–23. But God also forgave David.

Do you have any sin-fected areas of your life you've been making worse with your lies and evasions? Don't let another day go by without confessing these sins and telling the truth—to yourself, to God, and to others.

Today's Takeaways

- *A wound grows worse with a lack of truth.* Sin, like bacteria, grows in dark, damp places. John 3:20 declares, "For everyone who does wicked things hates the light and does not come to the light, lest his works should be exposed" (ESV). For a "sin-fection," be sure to shine the light of God's grace and truth on it, then sprinkle on a salty confession. Jesus is the only way we can have forgiveness.

- *Don't pour.* In cooking, the only time you pour salt

on something is when you are ruining it! Have you ever seen a Food Network chef take the canister of salt and just start pouring it onto a dish? No, because that is about the fastest way to destroy a recipe. In the same manner, frantically pouring lies, distractions, and selfish choices onto a situation will ruin *you* just as fast.

- *God can redeem the ruined.* Some things seem past recovery, but not in God's eyes. This situation with Bathsheba seemed utterly ruined by David's actions, but God had a plan. Through Bathsheba and David's descendants came Jesus. You never know how the salty words of confession will heal your heart and allow God to change a recipe from unredeemable to glorious.

Lesson for the Lips

Confess your sin. Right. Now. Really! First John 1:9 urges, "If we confess our sins, he is faithful and just to forgive us our sins and to cleanse us from all unrighteousness" (ESV). Read Psalm 51. This is David's earnest prayer of confession, and we can pray it right along with him. Or just pray verse 10, which begs, "Create in me a clean heart, O God, and renew a right spirit within me" (ESV). On a sheet of paper, pen a prayer of confession to God. Read it out loud to him. Then tear it up and toss it into the trash, knowing your sins are forgiven.

Prayer

Dear heavenly Father, please help me admit when I am wrong. Remind me that the truth will set me free. Let me always make decisions of integrity, but if I don't, help me to confess my sin immediately so my heart can be clean again. Let me add the salty words of confession to my daily spiritual vocabulary. Save me from the debilitating infection of multiple sins by staying constantly in your sight. Help me to daily speak the truth and always look to you to make good decisions in the first place. In Jesus's name, amen.

33

IT ALL HAPPENED SO FAST: THE SWEET WORDS OF BOAZ

"Lie down until the morning." (Ruth 3:13 ESV)

You know that moment when one thing has led to another, everything is kind of a blur, and it all happened so fast?

Maybe there was an argument when you said something harsh "in the moment" instead of thinking through your response. Or perhaps you agreed to prepare a meal for a new mom or signed up for a ministry at church without fully evaluating the commitment.

Sometimes we say yes to something because—at the time—it seems like the only response to a few seconds of verbal pressure or those pleading puppy dog eyes. However, "yes" and "no" are not the only conversational exits to weighty requests. When a situation is rapidly moving in one direction, your words don't have to. What if we took our cues from Boaz?

Boaz was a relative of Naomi and a "worthy man," as

Ruth 2:1 says (ESV). Naomi was Ruth's mother-in-law and Ruth was a beautiful widow who worked in Boaz's fields collecting grain. Boaz looked out for Ruth, gave her food, and made sure she had plenty of grain to take back to Naomi. In other words, she caught his eye.

Then one night Naomi suggested Ruth go lie down at Boaz's feet. Ruth went to Boaz after he had eaten and drunk and "his heart was merry" (Ruth 3:7 ESV).

Did you catch that? Boaz was alone with a single woman and already in a happy mood. Things could have "happened so fast" in this situation. But they didn't. Why?

Well, one reason may have been Boaz's sweet words. They were *not* the sweet nothings a man uses to woo a lady, but the sweet advice of wisdom and patience.

Ruth wanted Boaz to redeem her by becoming her husband. However, Boaz had already researched the matter and knew he was not the first in line for this lovely lady. He said,

> "May you be blessed by the LORD, my daughter. You have made this last kindness greater than the first in that you have not gone after young men, whether poor or rich. And now, my daughter, do not fear. I will do for you all that you ask, for all my fellow townsmen know that you are a worthy woman. And now it is true that I am a redeemer. Yet there is a redeemer nearer than I. Remain tonight, and in the morning, if he will redeem you, good; let him do it. But if he is not willing to redeem you, then, as the

LORD lives, I will redeem you. Lie down until the morning" (Ruth 3:10–13 ESV).

Wasn't that tender? I am so amazed at Boaz's self-control, thoughtfulness, and overall sweetness. Maybe (and perhaps it's a bit far-fetched) this was the first biblical account of someone saying, "Let me sleep on it." (Hey, you never know.)

By waiting until morning, Boaz was able to clearly and legally sort things out with the other man. He used his words wisely the next day, and in the end was able to redeem and marry Ruth. Then, at the sweet and appropriate time, Ruth and Boaz were able to . . . well . . . have some *horizontal fellowship* as man and wife. ;-)

And it did not happen too fast or in a dishonoring way. It happened in a God's-perfect-timing kind of way.

Today's Takeaways

- *Slow speech pairs well with slow actions.* There's definitely a time to act fast, like when someone is hurt or there's a great deal on your favorite laundry detergent. But more often than not, we all need to *sloooooooow* down. "Do you see a man who is hasty in his words? There is more hope for a fool than for him" (Prov. 29:20 ESV).

- *Follow through.* We shouldn't go around giving a bunch of people answers like "maybe" or "I'll get back to you" and be so slow that weeks go by and we are never clear with our answers. Boaz said he would handle it the next morning. And he did.

- *Have dessert first.* In Day 31 of this challenge we noticed how Abigail started out with humble words and how humility is a good starter. Being sweet is also a delightful way to start a reply. It helps cushion or prepare listeners, while also letting them know how much you care about them.

Lesson for the Lips

Look up Proverbs 15:28 and jot it down on a sticky note or note card. Then keep it in a place where you will see it before falling asleep at night. This will help you remember (as it does for me) that not every response needs to happen in the heat of the moment. Words can wait until morning. Decisions can wait until morning. Commitments can wait until they've been properly evaluated and prayed over.

Prayer

Dear heavenly Father, please help me weigh my words carefully. Allow me to have wise, tender, and patient responses in situations that could easily escalate into sin. Please help me put into practice the art of speaking God-honoring words at God-appointed times. In Jesus's name, amen.

34

KICKING IT UP A NOTCH: THE SALTY WORDS OF MORDECAI

He sent back this answer: "Do not think that
because you are in the king's house you alone
of all the Jews will escape." (Est. 4:13)

When pregnant with our third child, I was on a quest to discover baby names that began with "M." Already the mom of Mackenzie and Mitchell, I thought we should keep up the alliteration when naming our darling dependents. I came up with several female names we liked, but I was at a loss for male versions. And so we brought baby #3 home from the hospital unnamed. Finally, on the last day allowed by our state, we chose to break tradition and call him Spencer. Too bad I didn't think of Mordecai.

Have you ever met someone named Mordecai? Well, me neither, but I do have some great friends who act like a

Mordecai in my life. What I mean by that is, a friend who really knows how to kick it up a notch.

A Mordecai is a friend who gives you a little salty encouragement. Their advice to you is truthful, loving, and mixed with divine reminders. A Mordecai is a valuable friend to have on your spice rack of soul sisters.

The original man Mordecai comes from the book of Esther. Esther was Mordecai's cousin. However, he had raised her as his own daughter. She—through the course of winning a beauty pageant of Persian sorts—was now the queen. Mordecai had truly watched her grow: "Every day he walked back and forth near the courtyard of the harem to find out how Esther was and what was happening to her" (Est. 2:11). (Why, he probably followed her every move on Instagram!)

An enemy of the Jews named Haman devised a plan to kill all of God's chosen people. He convinced the king to sign a decree with instructions to annihilate the Jews. Mordecai went to the palace gates and sent a messenger to Esther with a copy of the decree. Mordecai told her "to go into the king's presence to beg for mercy and plead with him for her people" (Est. 4:8).

Esther sent a message back to Mordecai that said, "All the king's officials and the people of the royal provinces know that for any man or woman who approaches the king in the inner court without being summoned the king has but one law: that they be put to death unless the king extends the gold scepter to them and spares their lives. But thirty days have passed since I was called to go to the king" (Est. 4:11).

Instead of gently molly-coddling Esther or being hazy in

his advice, Mordecai got down to business and gave her some salty speech.

He said, "Do not think that because you are in the king's house you alone of all the Jews will escape. For if you remain silent at this time, relief and deliverance for the Jews will arise from another place, but you and your father's family will perish. And who knows but that you have come to your royal position for such a time as this?" (Est. 4:13–14).

These words from Mordecai are famous, but the next words spoken by Esther are just as significant: "If I perish, I perish" (Est. 4:16). I have to wonder if it was Mordecai's words—or the man behind them—that gave Esther her courage.

After fasting and praying, Esther approached the king, made him aware of Haman's intentions, and ultimately saved her people by bravely risking her own life. The king did not put Esther to death, but instead had Haman killed. It's a remarkable story of courage.

Don't miss out on having a Mordecai in your life. She doesn't have to carry that exact name, but she does have to love you well enough to remind you that everything isn't about you.

And who knows but that God might be calling you to be a Mordecai to a certain friend at such a time as this.

Today's Takeaways

- *Encouragement can't forget the courage.* Encouragement that's nice without a purpose is flattery. Encouragement to impart courage to the recipient is love.

- *Marinate in love.* Salty words are discarded—or even damaging—if the relationship hasn't first had a long soak in the juices of trust and love. Don't attempt salting without a proven history of loving.

- *Don't fix it and forget it.* Don't give salty encouragement to friends without following up or sticking with them. Esther said to fast and pray for three days, and that's what Mordecai did too. He was loyal to her. Don't speak your mind to friends and then neglect to walk through the tough situation right along with them. Stick closer than a brother . . . or . . . um . . . sister (Prov. 18:24).

Lesson for the Lips

Here is a verse to make into a screen saver for your phone, tablet, or computer: "Let no corrupting talk come out of your mouths, but only such as is good for building up" (Eph. 4:29 ESV). Salty encouragement is never mean-spirited or destructive. Whether our words are sweet or salty, the end result should work toward building each other up. I challenge you to give salty encouragement to others only in love, not in jealousy. In person. Online. And on the phone. Salt is strong; use it wisely and sparingly!

Prayer

Dear heavenly Father, the rest of Ephesians 4:29 says I should talk in a way that "fits the occasion, that it may give grace to those who hear." Lord, only you can help me discern how much salt to use in encouraging my sisters and brothers. Let me always speak from a heart of love. Let me marinate myself in your Word to speak true encouragement to others. In Jesus's name, amen.

35

SOUL FOOD: THE SWEET AND SALTY WORDS OF JESUS

"Zacchaeus, hurry and come down, for I must
stay at your house today." (Luke 19:5 ESV)

When was the last time you took a bite of something so sensational, so exquisite, so ravishing in its flavor that you involuntarily said "Wow!" after the first bite? It was moist, but not sticky, creamy but not heavy, rich but not overpowering. It was—with no exaggeration—perfect. Perhaps this edible masterpiece was so good that, even by the end of your portion, those last few bites possessed the same wonder and delight as the first!

It is with this savory nostalgia that I can best describe the delectable words of Jesus. He wasn't always sweet, and he wasn't always salty, but somehow he knew the perfect blend.

Zacchaeus would tell you this. I'm anticipating your look of confusion and saying, "Zacchaeus? Really!" Yes, the short guy who climbed a tree and has a catchy little Sunday school song written after him. I believe Zacchaeus tasted both the sweet and the salty words of Jesus.

The story of Zacchaeus in Luke 19 is brief and simple. Zacchaeus wants to see Jesus, but can't because he's too short to see over the crowd. Zacchaeus climbs a tree. Jesus says something. Zacchaeus says something. Jesus says something. Done.

But hold your horses just a minute. *Their exchange needs to be savored.*

Zacchaeus was up in the tree, and when Jesus spotted him, he said, "Zacchaeus, hurry and come down, for I must stay at your house today" (v. 5 ESV).

Jesus said his name. Jesus gave him a command. Jesus invited himself to dinner. It's salty to invite yourself to someone's house for dinner, it's salty to tell them what to do, and it's really salty to do both those things in your very first sentence to a stranger!

But that's just the thing. Zacchaeus wasn't a stranger to Jesus. Jesus knew his name. Jesus knew Zacchaeus wanted nothing more than to have Jesus to dinner. And Jesus knew that despite being hidden by crowds, all Zacchaeus really wanted was to be *found* and to be *saved.*

So after Jesus's first words, Zacchaeus "came down at once and welcomed him gladly" (v. 6). Some nearby haters muttered that because Zacchaeus was a tax collector who bilked people out of their hard-earned money, he was a sinner. But confronted with Jesus's love and mercy, Zacchaeus had a change of heart and wanted to prove it through his actions. So he told Jesus, "Look, Lord! Here and now I give half of my possessions to the poor, and if I have cheated anybody out of anything, I will pay back four times the amount" (v. 8). And Jesus replied, "Today salvation has come to this house, because this man, too, is a son of Abraham. For the Son of Man came to seek and to save the lost" (vv. 9–10).

Isn't it completely marvelous how Zaccheus was talking about money and Jesus was talking about salvation? Zaccheus *uttered* something. Jesus's words *accomplished* something. Zaccheus's words were for ears, but Jesus's words were for the heart.

No words taste as good as those said to a starving soul.

Has it been a while since you've tasted those words?

His words are sweet because they save us. His words are salty because they tell us what we need to hear. His words are alive because the Bible tells us so (Heb. 4:12).

We need to use words like Jesus used them—as *soul food*. Sweet, salty, rich, creamy, exquisite, inspiring, aromatic . . . *Life-changing*.

Jesus comes to save the lost. And he wants to come over to your house today.

What do you say?

Today's Takeaways

- *Less is more*. In this passage of Scripture, Jesus says three sentences to Zaccheus. Let your words be few and meaningful. Quantity doesn't add meaning. Use quality ingredients.

- *Go with the brand name*. Use people's names when

you address them. This lets them know you really know them. It's respectful. And it lets the other person know you cared enough to remember who they are.

- *Create a pleasant aftertaste.* Leave your listeners with deep and sweet words that will uplift them whenever their minds replay them. Your words may linger longer than you know. Make them life-giving.

Lesson for the Lips

Invite Jesus into your life today. Maybe you have acknowledged that he died on the cross for your sins and maybe you are living in this forgiveness and grace, but do you consistently taste the sweet and salty words of Jesus? Did you consume his Word today? What if you read the Bible at one meal each day? Read a few verses. Think about them. Eat some delicious food and see if you enjoy having Jesus over for breakfast, lunch, or dinner!

Prayer

Dear heavenly Father, your Word says, "Oh, taste and see that the LORD is good!" (Ps. 34:8 ESV). Let me taste the words of your Son and let them nourish my spirit. Let me get to where I can hear you, listen to you, and be changed by you. Let me speak words of life to others, as your Son has given us the perfect example. I pray that I hunger for you. In Jesus's name, amen.

How God's Words
Affect Our Words

36

GOD'S WORD TEACHES US HOW TO RESPOND WITH FORGIVENESS

Peter came to Jesus and asked, "Lord, how many times
shall I forgive my brother or sister who sins against me?
Up to seven times?" Jesus answered, "I tell you, not seven
times, but seventy-seven times." (Matt. 18:21–22)

I was with a friend at a coffee shop recently. She was discussing a dilemma she had with a coworker who wasn't doing her job. Now, my friend wasn't gossiping or being malicious; she was honestly asking for some advice with how to move forward with a particular coworker. The person she described was kind and attentive outside of work but wouldn't finish tasks when clocked in. She looked at me and said, "Karen, how am I supposed to respond to all this?"

"Have you been patient with her?" I asked.

"Of course."

"Have you clearly explained your expectations to her?"

"Yes."

"Have you outlined the consequences if she fails to meet these expectations?"

My friend let out an exasperated sigh. "Yes, and she still won't do as I ask!"

We continued to brainstorm possible solutions to her workplace woes, and I concluded that for now, graciousness and patience would be the best response.

Oh, how I wish I had taken my own advice!

Because afterward, it just so happened—in a God coincidence kind of way—that I went home after that coffee time and found out about a serious disappointment from someone in my own life. I didn't respond the best way. At the time, I felt like this was "the last straw!" Though my delivery might have been in a calm tone, I was unforgiving and unyielding. Had I clearly defined my expectations to this person? No. Had I told this person what the consequences would be if this behavior continued? Um, no. Had I been gracious and patient with this person? Nuh-uh. You see, like most if not all of us, I am better at giving advice than I am at living that advice out in reality!

Not only that, but in small group earlier that week, our group leader had said, "Today we are talking about how many times we should forgive." In those two instances—in my coffee time and in small group—God directly spoke to me and laid out the recipe for how I should respond to the difficult situation I faced soon after. But in the heat of the moment I blew it.

In Matthew 18 Jesus tells the parable of the unforgiving servant. Within this parable are four specific descriptions for what we should do when we are in a position to forgive.

1. Respond with mercy. The parable consists of a king who wanted to settle his accounts. He realized a man owed him a large sum of money, so he demanded the debtor sell his possessions and pay the amount owed. The debtor "fell on his knees before him. 'Be patient with me,' he begged, 'and I will pay back everything'" (v. 26). The king took pity on him, was merciful, and canceled his debt.

2. Be willing to forgive. The king forgave the debtor and released him. But when this newly forgiven man was free, he found his own servant and began demanding a much smaller amount of debt be paid. His servant begged him for patience, but this forgiven man "wasn't willing," as verse 30 of the Holman Christian Standard Bible puts it.

3. Draw upon the mercy of Christ. When the king found out what had happened, he questioned the man. "Shouldn't you have had mercy on your fellow servant just as I had on you?" (v. 33). The forgiven man should have remembered the mercy he received and then extended that same mercy to the one who had wronged him.

4. Be sincere. The king threw the unforgiving debtor into prison until he could repay his debt. Jesus concludes the entire parable by saying, "This is how my heavenly Father will treat each of you unless you forgive your brother or sister from your heart" (v. 35).

I have lived this parable out on a few occasions, particularly this time with my friend at the coffee shop. In my mind I was thinking all she had to do was be more gracious, but then when I was in the very same position, I found it hard to be gracious and forgiving.

If I was right back at the coffee shop with my friend as she asked me, "How am I supposed to respond to all this?" I would answer, "We need to pray and find strength to forgive as the Lord has forgiven us." And then when I encountered my own disappointment with someone, I would also pray for patience and mercy.

Maybe we haven't been lazy at work, but we have sinned in other ways. When we consider how many times we have asked for forgiveness in *any* area, only then are we able to properly see that we have been forgiven more times than we could ever count. We have been forgiven seventy times seven, which is why we can respond with that Jesus-kind-of-forgiveness toward others.

Today's Takeaways

- *Keep no record.* We tend to keep score in relationships. This isn't biblical, though. First Corinthians 13:5

says love "keeps no record of wrongs." It will be easier for us to forgive when we aren't tabulating the other person's offenses. If we haven't been mentally keeping score, then we won't bring them up when the time comes to forgive.

- *Forgive as the Lord forgave you.* Whenever someone has wronged you, just bring this simple phrase to mind: "Forgive as the Lord forgave you" (Col. 3:13). Patience and forgiveness are not always easy to extend, but remembering God's patience with us will motivate us to show forbearance.

Lesson for the Lips

Simply remember "Forgive as the Lord forgave you" and let it be a phrase that stays in your mind and on your lips.

You know those cute pictures with inspirational phrases all over social media? Make your own artwork below. If you aren't much for drawing, then simply write the phrase. But if you'd like, creatively use some colored pencils or markers to write "Forgive as the Lord forgave you" in the space provided.

_____

_____

_____

_____

_____

_____

Prayer

Dear heavenly Father, my prayer is so simple today. I ask that whenever I am in a position to forgive, I will remember how you respond to us when we ask for forgiveness. Allow me a good memory of your mercy and a sincere heart and willingness to extend that grace to others. I want to respond to people patiently and mercifully. In Jesus's name, amen.

37

GOD'S WORD TEACHES US HOW TO RESPOND IN PRAYER

"And will not God bring about justice for his chosen
ones, who cry out to him day and night? Will he
keep putting them off? I tell you, he will see that
they get justice, and quickly." (Luke 18:7–8)

I'd like to think that, for most of my childhood, I truly abided
by my home's rules and expectations. If Mom made it clear
I couldn't go somewhere or hang out with a certain group
of friends, I tried to honor her wishes. My friend Lindsey
and I were talking about this the other day. She told me she
behaved the same way. Well, except one time when the giant
roller coasters were calling her name.

It was the summer after she received her driver's license.
She had her own car and was ridiculously excited about the
possibility of spreading her wings and taking a day trip with
friends. A theme park in Ohio was not too far from where we

lived, and going there seemed like the perfect first trip. She started by asking her parents for permission casually. They said no. She asked the next day with a little more seriousness. They said no again. The third day she decided to give it a rest. On the fourth day she decided to pull on their emotions by expressing her deep desire to make this trip happen. Day five began with a slew of facts outlining why it would be a great trip and how it would develop her into a more responsible driver. The week went on as she employed random advertising methods, pleas like "I'll pay for gas," and pretty much anything else she could think of to get her parents to allow this fantastic trip.

I have to hand it to her parents; they were pretty patient through the whole thing. But by about day ten, they finally got tired of her talking and decided to let her go.

She did end up going, and yet she says, "To be quite honest, I felt sort of let down. I felt remorse for putting my parents through all the hardship. Sure, it was a nice time, but I couldn't quite remember why I had wanted to go so badly in the first place. At some point in the pleading process with them, I think I forgot what I was fighting for and simply wanted to win the persuasion battle we were having."

I thought about Lindsey's teenage travel story as I read the story of the persistent widow. Here it is, from Luke 18:2–8:

> "In a certain town there was a judge who neither feared God nor cared what people thought. And there was a widow in that town who kept coming to him with the plea, 'Grant me justice against my

adversary.' For some time he refused. But finally he said to himself, 'Even though I don't fear God or care what people think, yet because this widow keeps bothering me, I will see that she gets justice, so that she won't eventually come and attack me!' And the Lord said, 'Listen to what the unjust judge says. And will not God bring about justice for his chosen ones, who cry out to him day and night? Will he keep putting them off? I tell you, he will see that they get justice, and quickly. However, when the Son of Man comes, will he find faith on the earth?'"

As I read this passage, I see how the widow had a good reason to continue going to the judge. When I think about my friend pleading with her parents, I realize her motivations were definitely not nearly as noble as the widow's were. This woman was seeking justice. Sometimes we get fired up about human trafficking, political injustice, or even friends who need healing, but do we sustain our prayers toward heaven with the same kind of fervor this woman possessed? This is hard to do unless we feel passionately about those situations. I think before we can produce God-honoring words in any of our prayers, we must possess a heart filled with compassion for the needs we are bringing before the Father.

If we as teens can be that persistent about something so minuscule and fleeting as a car trip, what kind of power do we have as women to be persistent about serious matters, especially those that affect eternity?

Today's Takeaways

- *Fight the good fight.* When using our words to do battle in prayer, let us not fight for selfish aspirations or temporary wins. Let us use our words to do battle for the friend who is in the hospital with cancer. Let us use our words to do battle for the family at church struggling financially. Let us use words to battle for our pastor not to grow weary in preaching the Word in season and out. Let our words matter and, even more, let the fights we fight in prayer be meaningful and not frivolous.

- *Use various tools.* When Lindsey was pleading with her parents, she kept approaching the trip from different angles. Some days she laid out the facts and other days she unashamedly begged. I think we have to use our words in various strategic ways when we go before God. Pray in any and all ways.

Lesson for the Lips

Write down one thing you would like to be persistent about in prayer today. Ask God to give you passion. Every time you think about this thing, shoot up a prayer. Try for all of today and tonight to pray about it from different angles. See what

God might teach you about persistence. What is the one persistent prayer you have today? Record it here:

_____

_____

_____

_____

Prayer

*Dear heavenly Father, allow me to be passionate
about the people and problems around me that
matter most. Give me persistence. Help me use words
that present my prayer request from different angles.
Help me grow in love for those I pray for. Most of all,
I pray you will answer the specific prayers I bring
before you today in faith. In Jesus's name, amen.*

38

GOD'S WORD TEACHES US HOW TO RESPOND IN FAITH

The centurion replied, "Lord, I do not deserve to
have you come under my roof. But just say the word,
and my servant will be healed." (Matt. 8:8)

I've never met anyone who has seen the classic family movie *Mary Poppins* and not enjoyed it. Talented actors, beautiful voices, and an amusing plotline—there's something for everyone. What's not to love?

One of my favorite scenes is when the kids have to clean up the messy nursery. Mary Poppins sings a little song instructing them to snap their fingers. In some impressive special effects for the time, all the clothing and toys go right back to where they belong as Jane and Michael snap along to a catchy tune.

For years after seeing the movie, my friends and I would

talk about how we wished we could merely snap our fingers and clean up messes. Or if the snapping thing was a bust, maybe we could be granted a nanny who possessed the snapping power and was "practically perfect in every way."

We never did have a nanny who was nearly perfect, but God did give me a completely perfect Savior in his Son, Jesus Christ.

Jesus had to clean up a lot of messes while he was here on earth. They might not have looked like toys strewn across the floor or loose laundry draped on bedposts, but Jesus had to clean up a lot of ugly spaces in our human hearts.

Throughout the New Testament we see Jesus healing people in a variety of ways. For almost all situations, Jesus was present with the person who needed to be healed. But then we have the story of the Roman centurion.

This Roman centurion came to Jesus and pleaded for his paralyzed servant to be healed. Jesus offered to visit his house to heal the servant, but the Roman centurion gave an epic response. "Lord, I do not deserve to have you come under my roof. But just say the word, and my servant will be healed" (Matt. 8:8).

The Bible says Jesus was amazed by his faith. What a response! Not only is the response of the Roman centurion remarkable, but it's also remarkable that Jesus would be amazed by someone's faith.

We see in Genesis how God creates water, plants, stars, and living creatures just with the words that come from his mouth. Here in Matthew 8 we see this indelible example of

Jesus using his *words* to heal someone without even being physically present. This is an amazing glimpse at how powerful the words of Jesus our Savior really are.

It takes me back to God creating the stars. When he created the stars, they didn't say, "Will you please put me over there?" or "Actually, I want to shine a more bluish light, if possible," or "I was hoping I could be a bigger star and not so small." It didn't go like that. When God created the stars and told them to shine, they just listened. They started shining. And they never stopped. It was as if there was nothing inside of them going against what God said. They obeyed and they kept obeying. You can look up into the sky tonight and see those same obedient stars peeking through obedient clouds in the obedient sky. Tomorrow night you'll see the same thing.

I think that's what happened with the Roman centurion. I believe he was willing to have God's word go through him with nothing stopping it. He had faith Jesus could do this work, and he had faith Jesus's word was powerful enough. Because it is.

The example from *Mary Poppins* is whimsical. I realize that. It really is nothing like the power Jesus has. With him, there are no special effects or catchy tunes. All we find with a person who is willing to believe anything is possible with God is an extraordinary power coming into effect.

Jesus doesn't have to be physically with someone to perform a healing. All we need is his word. All we need is to ask with faith like the Roman centurion did.

Today's Takeaways

- *Keep shining.* When God told the stars to shine, they never got a second order, so they just kept on doing what he originally told them to do! I love that thought, don't you? Sometimes when I tire of an ongoing responsibility I know God has called me to fulfill, I pray this prayer of recommitment: "Lord, I'm going to keep on doing this until I hear otherwise."

- *"Jesus, say the word."* Consider a friend you can't be physically present with right now but who needs healing. In yesterday's reading we talked about pleading with God. A few Bible translations say the Roman centurion actually *pleaded* with Jesus. Other translations use words like *appealed*, *beseeched*, or *implored*. Remember this: You don't have to be with your friend, and Jesus doesn't have to be physically present. You just have to faithfully ask and Jesus just has to "say the word."

Lesson for the Lips

Recognize the authority of Jesus (Matthew 8:9-10). Remember that his Word will not return void (Isaiah 55:11). Realize it could happen in a moment (Matthew 8:13). In the space below, provide one memory of something you brought before the Lord in prayer for a long time and then God answered in a moment.

_____

_____

_____

_____

Prayer

Dear heavenly Father, I want to respond with words of faith that amaze you! Let the words I speak to others and to you be words that reflect my acknowledgment of your authority. Thank you for this example and thank you for showing us what a faithful response looks like. Help me to put into practice what I've learned here today. Allow me to shine and to continue shining at your command. In Jesus's name, amen.

39

GOD'S WORD TEACHES US HOW TO RESPOND COMPASSIONATELY

"But the father told his slaves, 'Quick! Bring out the best robe and put it on him; put a ring on his finger and sandals on his feet.'" (Luke 15:22 HCSB)

In my sophomore year of college, as I was driving back to my dorm after an afternoon of shopping in the city, a car's driver ran a stop sign and smashed into the side of my 1979 Oldsmobile Vista Cruiser station wagon. Uninjured but upset, I got out of my car and discovered the person who hit me was someone I knew: the college baseball coach's teenage daughter.

She was understandably shaken. And because she was driving a nearly new car, not an old clunker like mine, she was apprehensive about calling her parents. But with a little encouragement she walked to a building on campus to phone her dad. As soon as she explained that she was in a car accident, her dad asked over and over again, "How are you? Are you safe? Do you have any injuries at all? Are you sure you're okay?"

She confessed the accident was all her fault. She expressed her concern about the vehicle, but repeatedly her dad's only concern was whether she was safe. He reassured her he didn't care about the car.

As I remember that incident, it touches my heart. My kids have been in minor accidents, and I have certainly been more concerned about their well-being above the car, but in this particular situation I might have had a hard time looking past the price tag of that nice vehicle. A lot of the cars we've owned have been bargains from Craigslist or grandparents' hand-me-downs. Would I still be so concerned about my kids if I had just recently laid down a large sum of money to buy a brand-new vehicle? Even if insurance covered the cost of repairs, the car would never be the same.

I see one similarity between this story and the story of the prodigal son. Don't get ahead of me; this girl didn't deliberately hurt her father, squandering what he had given her to use as the prodigal squandered what his father had given him. As far as I know, she just made an honest mistake as an inexperienced driver. She wasn't estranged from her father. She hadn't left her family to pursue a life of pleasure. No, none of those things are what I see in common with the parable of the prodigal son.

The similarity I see is in the fathers. Both the girl and the son had a dad who responded to the bigger picture.

In both verses 24 and 32 of Luke 15 we read that the father says of the son, "He was lost and is found!" The son, who had selfishly taken all of his inheritance from his father early, was now back home to confess he had been foolish. And amazingly, the father responds with joy! No bitterness. No guilt trips. The father didn't look at his clothes and remark on his shabby appearance. In that moment the father was able to step back and see the big picture of his son's homecoming. *Two times* within this parable we see the father use the same joyous phrase: "He was lost and is found!"

Not only that, but the father says, "Quick! Bring out the best robe and put it on him" (v. 22).

The Bible is so practical. What if I used those same words when someone came to me admitting their faults? Take a moment to think about what it would look like to respond to a desperately repentant person by saying, "Quick! Let me get my very best for you." Picture *yourself* saying those words to someone.

"Quick! Let me get my very best for you."

Then picture *yourself* receiving those words.

"Quick! Let me get my very best for you."

The father who was more concerned with his daughter's well-being than the damage to the car is a great reminder to look at the big picture. The prodigal's father gives us the idea of "bringing out the best." Both are beautiful aspects of delivering compassionate responses.

Are you challenged by this? Let's consider a couple of takeaways from today's reading.

Today's Takeaways

- *Don't wait for the magic words.* Some people are more sincere in their apologies than others. Some people give apologies that almost don't sound like apologies at all. But we are only responsible for our response. Don't wait for an enchanting combination of words. The Bible says, "While the son was still a long way off, his father saw him and was filled with compassion. He ran, threw his arms around his neck, and kissed him. The son said to him, 'Father, I have sinned against heaven and in your sight. I'm no longer worthy to be called your son'" (Luke 15:20–21 HCSB). The son didn't even have a chance to formulate a worthy response. The father was already hugging and kissing him, letting him know he accepted him. What an example!

- *Bring out the best.* Very simply, use your words to display lavish compassion. Don't hesitate. Do it quickly. What an expression of love it will be.

Lesson for the Lips

Think of a person who is currently disappointing you. Ask God to help you write down a premeditated response of compassion. Keep in mind what we talked about today and ask Jesus to guide your words. Write your grace-filled response here:

_____

_____

_____

_____

Prayer

Dear heavenly Father, thank you for being a Father who receives us with open arms. Thank you for showing us how to love like you love. Thank you for showing us how to respond like you in situations we will eventually face. I pray that when the time comes, I will look at the big picture and bring out the best words I've taken time to store up in my heart. In Jesus's name, amen.

40

GOD'S WORD TEACHES US HOW TO RESPOND TO PROBLEMS

Hezekiah received the letter from the messengers
and read it. Then he went up to the temple of the Lord
and spread it out before the Lord. (2 Kings 19:14)

Here we are on Day 40! Thank you for your consistency.
Thank you for your patience and attentive heart. How I wish
I could sit down with you and talk about all we have learned
together. Instead I will leave you with one last story from the
Bible. This story is from 2 Kings 19. I love this story, and I
hope it penetrates your heart the same way it does mine.

Each of us faces problems every day. They can be as simple
as losing our car keys to as devastating as receiving an unfavorable
diagnosis from the doctor. When we receive unpleasant news,
where do we go? Who do we talk to? How do we process it?

In 2 Kings 19 we have the story of King Hezekiah of Judah coming under attack. The king of Assyria sends someone to scare the people and tell Hezekiah he shouldn't trust God. Here are the actual words of his threat:

> "Do not let the god you depend on deceive you when he says, 'Jerusalem will not be given into the hands of the king of Assyria.' Surely you have heard what the kings of Assyria have done to all the countries, destroying them completely. And will you be delivered? Did the gods of the nations that were destroyed by my predecessors deliver them . . . ?" (vv. 10–12)

The king of Assyria goes on to name the gods of other nations that were not able to protect their nation from destruction.

Hezekiah's response is unforgettable. "Hezekiah received the letter from the messengers and read it. Then he went up to the temple of the LORD and spread it out before the LORD" (v. 14). Next, Hezekiah says one of the most heartfelt and beautiful prayers of the Bible.

> "LORD, the God of Israel, enthroned between the cherubim, you alone are God over all the kingdoms of the earth. You have made heaven and earth. Give ear, LORD, and hear; open your eyes, LORD, and see; listen to the words Sennacherib has sent to ridicule the living God. It is true, LORD, that the Assyrian kings have laid waste these nations and their lands. They have thrown their gods into the fire and destroyed them, for they

were not gods but only wood and stone, fashioned by human hands. Now, LORD our God, deliver us from his hand, so that all the kingdoms of the earth may know that you alone, LORD, are God." (vv. 15–19)

This passage gives us three things to remember when responding to a problem.

1. **Go to God first**. Hezekiah went directly to the Lord. It's so simple, isn't it? It's an astounding reality that we can go to him at any time. We have an all-access pass through Jesus Christ to go to our heavenly Father in an office, in a car, or while we are hiding from our biggest fears. He is there and we just need to go to him first.

2. **Lay it all out**. I have this picture in my mind of Hezekiah taking the message and unrolling it on a table in the temple. I picture his hands spreading the entire paper flat and smoothing out the wrinkles or curled edges. I picture him looking at the message and then looking up, doing everything in his power to clearly show God precisely what he is facing.

3. **Say who God is**. We can often get distracted by asking, "Who do they think they are to say something like that?" Or we might say something like, "I don't have time for this" or "I'm better than this." These aren't the best responses either. The very best response is to take Hezekiah's cue and declare who God is, before presenting requests.

As we reach the close of this journey together, I pray we remember to spread out our problems before the Lord. By taking our issues before the Lord, we prove he is the only one who can supernaturally do something about them.

Today's Takeaways

- *Go to God first.* This concept has been repeated throughout this book because it will save you so much heartache. Although you may be tempted to pick up the phone and call your best friend, allow God to be the one you call first. Practice this and see how he moves on your behalf.

- *Spread out the entire problem to God in prayer.* Don't give God the Twitter version of your problem. Sure, there are times for short prayers, but sometimes we need to flesh out the entire dilemma. Take time to describe the problem to God in its *entirety* and perhaps you will watch him answer it *entirely.* You will see the depth of his deliverance in all the details.

Lesson for the Lips

Below, map out, describe, or pick apart a problem in your life for the Lord to address. Start by confessing who God is. Then lay your requests out like Hezekiah did, spreading everything before the Lord.

_____

_____

_____

_____

_____

Prayer

Dear heavenly Father, no one is greater than you. Help me bring my problems to you before I share them with anyone else. I believe you can fix them more deeply, more truly, and more eternally than anyone else can. Thank you for this entire 40-day challenge. Help me to continue to honor you long after these forty days. Bring illustrations and takeaways to my mind at just the right time, for years to come. In Jesus's name, amen.

ACKNOWLEDGMENTS

To my Proverbs 31 Ministries sisters (and two brothers!), especially President Lysa TerKeurst: Serving God with you is my favorite thing to do! I love you all.

To Glynnis Whitwer and Steph Raquel: You help make devotion writing so much easier. Thank you.

To agent Esther Fedorkevich: Thank you for your encouragement and diligent work.

To my HarperCollins Christian Publishing family, especially Sandy Vander Zicht: Thank you for allowing me to turn my thoughts into books.

To Lori Vanden Bosch: Your keen editing skills and tweaking expertise is such a gift to me!

To Lindsey Feldpausch: Your biblical insight and help on this project is so appreciated! I love doing ministry with you.

To my husband, Todd, and children, Kenna, Mitchell, and Spencer: Thank you for your patience and encouragement whenever I work on a new book. This one was no exception.

To my Lord and Savior Jesus Christ: Thank you for dying on the cross for me, purchasing my way to heaven. Indescribable.